IN DEATH,
THE
GIFT OF LIFE

IN DEATH,
THE
GIFT OF LIFE

IN DEATH, THE THE GIFT OF LIFE

Inspired/Produced by
Dan Levinson
in honor of his father

Editor
Alison McBain

ISBN-13: 978-1-949122-16-9 (Paperback)
ISBN-13: 978-1-949122-17-6 (eBook)

Cover image and design by Miggs Burroughs.
Interior design by Alison McBain.

Fairfield Scribes—Fairfield, CT
WestportWRITES—Westport, CT
United States of America

First printing March 2020.
www.fairfieldscribes.com

Contents

PREFACE

This book is dedicated to my father, Dr. Peritz Levinson, who in his quiet, honest, steady way showed me how to live, and in whose thoughtful, intentional death was the gift of life.

—Dan Levinson

MY DAD'S LAST FEW MONTHS of life with me turned out to be one of the biggest gifts he ever gave me. Many people who experienced the beauty of that time said, "You have to share his story!"

While my father would never be interested in a book being written about him, once I started consulting with local experts, they all confirmed the value of talking about the way we consider illness and death. It made me realize that living well can also mean dying well, just as my father chose to experience it himself and share that experience with me. It seemed like an important conversation to open around a normally closed subject.

So I began to talk to others in my town of Westport, Connecticut. What started out as the kernel of an idea grew into a project bigger than just one story with one goal, and eventually became an all-community endeavor.

I'd like to thank the nationally recognized experts in their fields who run highly regarded programs in my hometown, and who became an invaluable part of this project from inception to conclusion. Thank you to Bill Harmer, Executive Director of the Westport Library; Sue Pfister, Executive Director of the Westport Center for Senior Activities; and Sharon Bradley, President & CEO of Visiting Nurse & Hospice of

Fairfield County. This project received further expert guidance from Westport's notable artist, Miggs Burroughs, and my long-time non-profit partner, Eileen Lavigne Flug.

I'd like to extend special thanks to the eleven local writers who penned the stories in this book: Dan Woog, Frank Hall & Lory Nurenberg, Craig D.B. Patton, Mary-Lou Weisman, Sheryl Kayne, Jonah Newman, Sarah Gross, Eleanor Duffy, Robin Weinberg, and Jarret Liotta. Jarret also deserves endless credit for working tirelessly behind a camera to produce the wonderful companion video to this anthology. We turned to another local, Alison McBain, lead editor of the small press Fairfield Scribes, who showed up with the experience, expertise, and heart to lead the charge and bring this project together.

We want to give the ten families within these pages our heartfelt thanks for sharing their stories and trusting us with their feelings and memories: Frank Hall & Lory Nurenberg, plus the families of Allen Wasserman, Estelle Margolis, Nancy Kuhn-Clark, Pamela Naughton, Anne C. Beers, Gerald Gross, Matthew Kleiner, and Charlie Karp.

In addition to everyone named here and in this book, I also want to extend a final thank you to all the partners, family members, writers, advisors, and others who have come together and worked behind the scenes with us to help bring this project to life.

We hope any reader at any age and from any place, near or far, can take inspiration and value from our work. Thank you for joining the conversation.

For more information about this subject, this anthology, or the team who brought this project to the page, all our community partners would welcome further discussion on this subject. If you'd like to reach out, please contact:

Sharon Bradley
Visiting Nurse & Hospice of Fairfield County
https://visitingnurse.net/

Bill Harmer
Westport Library
https://westportlibrary.org/

Sue Pfister
Westport Center for Senior Activities
https://www.westportct.gov/

We cannot see them
Transparent dragonfly wings
But we can all fly

—Diane Meyer Lowman
Poet Laureate of Westport, Connecticut

FOREWORD

I went to the woods because I wished to live deliberately, to front only the essential facts of life, and see if I could not learn what it had to teach, and not, when I came to die, discover that I had not lived.

—Thoreau, *Walden; or, Life in the Woods*

HENRY DAVID THOREAU BUILT A small cabin in the woods beside Walden Pond in Concord, Massachusetts, and he lived in it for two years, two months, and two days. He kept a journal, which he later published as a book. He said it was an experiment in simple living.

We, too, are engaged in a life; it's an experiment. Each of us is a unique individual and, like Thoreau, we want to know when we come to die that we have carved out a meaningful life from the cards we were dealt.

This collection is an expression of love . . . deliberately. It touches the heart of life.

The poet Stanley Kunitz affirms the examined life in a poem he entitled "The Layers." The opening lines put it well: "I have walked through many lives / some of them my own."

As we walk through life, we are changed by the people we meet; we are changed by the circumstances of our lives, the good fortunes and the mistakes and failures, and we make what Kunitz calls "a tribe / out of our true affections."

If we're fortunate, we make some lasting friends along the way: we connect. Then we suffer losses. As the poet Kunitz asks, "How shall the heart be reconciled / to its feast of losses?"

In Death, the Gift of Life is a collection of responses to this. Usually, we refer to a *feast* as indulging in a special meal in celebration of something or someone, but the "feast of losses" is not a joyous celebration; it's a celebration of another kind—the celebration of the life of one of our tribe, and the celebration of our connection to loved ones.

Our culture prescribes how to respond to the death of a loved one, planning a service, choosing a casket, and so forth. But there is a wide range of options to the traditional funeral and memorial services. When we plan a service to celebrate a life, we want it to be consistent with the real person's life; his/her beliefs, values, and dreams that were realized, and the ones that weren't.

In his book *Love and Will*, American existential psychologist Rollo May articulates the principle that an awareness of death is essential to life, rather than being opposed to life. He says that awareness of death is the primary ingredient of love; love is, in part, the consciousness that everything that lives will die someday, that it's all temporary.

In his book *The People, Yes*, the poet Carl Sandburg wrote, "Nothing more certain than death and nothing more uncertain than the hour."

The loss of a loved one is the source of grief, and grief can be complicated. The grief for a suicide, for example, may result in anger that invades the grieving. The death of a loved one who died a long, slow, painful death comes as a relief, which complicates the sense of loss when death finally arrives.

Early in my first ministry, I got a call from Grace, the wife of a long-term member. She asked me if I visited people in the hospital. I said I do, and she proceeded to tell me about her husband, Hiram: he was eighty-three years old and had just had surgery for cancer.

I went to visit him. I introduced myself as the minister of the Unitarian Church where he was an inactive member. He asked why I was visiting him, telling me that he hadn't been to the church "in a dog's age."

I asked if there was anything I could do for him.

He said, flatly, "No." There was a long pause, and then he said with an angry voice, "There *is* something you can do for me."

"What's that?" I asked.

"You can find out what's going on and tell me. I have a right to know."

"I'll talk to your wife," I said. He referred to her as "the Mrs."

His wife, Grace, said the surgeon told her that Hiram's cancer had spread and there was nothing to be done except keeping him as comfortable as possible.

She said, "I just couldn't bring myself to tell him what the doctor had said." I encouraged her to talk it through, and talk she did, reviewing their relationship and courtship and marriage. It was all in the affirmative.

Finally, I asked, "Would you like *me* to tell Hiram? He keeps saying, 'Why won't they tell me the truth?' He knows. He is very clear about wanting the truth."

She said she would appreciate it. When I visited him the next morning, he greeted me with a question: "What's the news?"

"It's not good." I explained what the doctor had told Grace.

He thanked me for "leveling" with him and offered his hand for a handshake. He held it for a longer time than usual.

"There is one thing you could do," he said. "I have four thousand dollars in cash, and it's yours if you will bring my gun."

I don't remember telling him that I couldn't do that, but he heard himself and answered his own question. It broke the silence; it started a deeply meaningful conversation between us.

His pain medication kicked in, and he started to doze off; I reached over and took his hand in a gesture of support. He gave me half a smile, and I told him I would see him tomorrow. I did, and I encouraged him to tell me his life story—at least, the chapter headings.

He had, by his own reckoning, a good life. I recognized the stages of his grief: he had pushed to get at the truth, to break through the denial about his medical situation. I admired him for his willingness to move through all the feelings of grief on short notice.

He had lived a good life, and now he was ready to die.

"My only regret," he said, "is leaving Grace." Those eyes weren't used to tears and, for the most part, he held them back.

I knew Hiram for only ten days, but sharing the final chapter of his life brought us close. On the tenth day, I walked up to the hospital reception desk to sign in, and the receptionist knew why I was there and told me that Hiram had *expired*. I asked where he was, and she told me he had *passed*. She hesitated to use the D-word. Giving in to it, she said simply, "He died . . . he's in ward X."

I told her I wanted to visit him. She called the nursing supervisor, who appeared quickly and invited me to come with her to the hospital morgue. She pulled out the drawer and unzipped the bag. I put my hand on his forehead, said my goodbye to Hiram, and thanked him for welcoming me into his life story.

I nodded to the supervisor; she zipped the bag and pushed the drawer back. Then she turned to me and asked carefully, "Can I ask you about what you did? Was it a religious ritual?"

I explained my need to see Hiram "at peace" after his suffering.

"I see," she said. She asked if I would speak to her nurses.

I suggested a brief talk, followed by an emphasis on their personal experiences with death and dying. I met with them three times, in a circle of sharing that was rich in stories about the deaths of hospital patients and the deaths of family members and friends.

The Greek playwright Aeschylus wrote, "*He who learns must suffer.* And even in our sleep, pain that cannot forget falls drop by drop upon the heart, and in our own despair, against our will, comes wisdom by the awful grace of God."

Suffering is a demanding teacher.

Elizabeth Kübler-Ross identified five stages of grief, which are now well-known and are sometimes thought to be hard and fast rules. In our own way, we experience phases of grief: denial, bargaining, anger, guilt, and acceptance. There is no timetable. No GPS to follow.

Grief is a natural response to a loss. The "stages" paradigm is simply a way of locating ourselves in a highly personal process. Such as poet Stanley Kunitz asking, "How shall the heart be reconciled / to its feast of losses?"

Twenty-seven years ago, I had a sabbatical and I decided to use the six months to explore the country. I bought my friend Mich's VW camper, and I lived in it for those six months by myself.

I went alone, looking for America and reconnecting with myself. I had no plan, but a few people offered suggestions of places to visit. One of those places was the Benedictine Monastery of Christ in the Desert in New Mexico.

Visitors were welcome. The monastery was at the end of a thirteen-mile dirt road with lots of rocks—it wasn't a casual drive, but a serious commitment and well worth the effort.

On the way into the chapel, there was an open grave. It didn't look freshly dug—it had a weathered feel to it. I asked Brother Andre, the monk who was in charge of making visitors feel welcome and understand the rules. He said matter-of-factly, "The open grave is a reminder that the next one could be for you." Its location near the entrance to the chapel, where the monks gathered several times a day for prayer, was a visible reminder of our fragile mortality.

The ten chapters in this collection illustrate aspects of letting go. They sing the praises of loved ones helping "the heart be reconciled / to its feast of losses." Whether it's loss of life, of health, of youth, or any other losses we endure.

The grief we experience makes us more human, more compassionate, kinder and more loving. Enter these stories and feel the simple and sacred connection to the life we share.

—Frank Hall
Minister Emeritus, Unitarian Church of Westport

FOREWORD

Peritz Levinson at his son's Westport, CT home (2018).

Raining Down Sunshine
•Peritz Levinson•

by Dan Woog

PERITZ LEVINSON HAD A LONG, exceptional life. A courtly, compassionate, and wise psychiatrist who loved his work and was beloved by his patients, he was healthy and clear-headed into his nineties. He was strongly involved in the world around him, and deeply interested in anyone whose path he crossed.

Peritz Levinson had a relatively short, wonderful death. He was peaceful and accepting, once the diagnosis of terminal cancer was confirmed. He spent his final three months dying, but also living. He inspired his family (old and young) and friends (old and new). His intention and clarity enabled all this.

In those last weeks, Peritz took his rich bond with his son to an even deeper level. Assisted by many others, Dan facilitated his father's choice of the gift of a good death. By himself—but never alone—Peritz gave Dan, and everyone in his son's orbit, the gift of how to live, and leave, a good life.

～⁂～

Peritz Levinson was born in 1928 in Cincinnati. To hear him tell it—and he enjoyed telling it—he had a nice, normal upbringing. He was a child of the Depression, but he did not grow up feeling deprived.

1

His father had Russian and German blood. He ran the Wyandot Cigar Factory in Cincinnati. His wife—Dan's grandmother—had a small "style shop." She helped ladies look and feel beautiful.

The football coach of his school wanted him to be a quarterback, but he preferred being a doctor to getting pummeled on the field. However, he was certainly an athlete. His sports were basketball and bodybuilding. Dan calls him "massive." When in high school, he used to tell his children that when young, his muscles were so big he couldn't scratch his own head—and had to ask friends to do so.

Peritz stayed close to home through medical school—the University of Cincinnati—and began his psychiatric practice there. He also lived in Texas for a stint as an Air Force doctor. He discovered golf there. "He loved golf before it was cool," says Dan.

When his parents grew ill, Peritz took care of them. But in the 1950s, he headed to New York City, the center of the North American psychiatric world.

He fell in love with a divorcee from Fall River, Massachusetts and now living in Manhattan. She had two very young children. They married; Peritz's wife's family included self-made businessmen and philanthropists. They were beautiful together, Dan says, and "seemed to make an awesome couple in the beginning. The early pictures are amazing."

Peritz loved psychiatry, and threw himself into his work. Back in New York, he saw thirty to forty patients a week. "He formed real relationships with many of them," Dan says. "He asked great questions."

Growing up, Dan did not always appreciate his father's "stability and thoughtfulness" as he navigated life with his wife and her family. Nor did he understand the "subtle giving-ness" that was part of the psychiatrist's professional demeanor.

Of course, Peritz did not talk about his patients—a wide variety, from high school students to older men and women—with his family. Instead, Dan says, he'd ask questions: "How are you doing? Are you getting enough sleep?" That was a way, Dan realizes now, for him to gain insights into his children. (Dan has an older sister, Deb, and a younger brother, Jon. In addition, Peritz adopted his wife's children from her previous marriage.)

Jo Ann List Levinson & Peritz Levinson, New York City (1960s).

Peritz worked closely with Dan on schoolwork and sports. He encouraged his son's interest in music, and—at their second home in the Berkshires—taught him to hike, camp, and make a fire. It was always "safety first" and manners, with Peritz and Dan always looking out for everyone else.

Dan grew up in 1960s New York, across from the 92nd Street YMCA. He remembers "lots of protests," for a variety of political issues. His parents went to museums and fundraisers, and hosted parties.

His mother was a "brilliant, gorgeous activist." But the stress of raising two children with mental illness—Dan's step-siblings—was tough. The couple separated in the early 1980s, after twenty-five years of marriage.

Around the same time, Peritz moved to Greenwich. Soon, he became a staff psychiatrist with Greenwich Hospital. The psychiatrist enjoyed "great relationships" with the doctors there. "It felt like home to him," Dan recalls.

Peritz continued his private practice, in two offices. He saw his longtime, devoted patients in New York, and new ones in Greenwich.

"He was a hard-core Freudian," Dan notes. "He wanted to be a blank slate. His offices were all beige."

But the American medical system was changing. New insurance regulations made it difficult to treat patients for the length of time psychiatrists were used to.

Despite those challenges, Peritz went to work eagerly every morning. He liked what he did, and was proud to do it. Even at eight-eight, he said, "As long as I keep awake, I'll keep working."

Outside of the office, Peritz was as interested in people as he was at work. He'd keep a social conversation going with a simple, "That's great to know!" He was non-judgmental, with a gift for making people feel comfortable, personally as well as professionally.

Besides his work, Peritz loved his children and grandchildren. He preached "living within our means," but was generous with gifts to his grandkids.

"He did not have big needs," Dan says. "Every weekend he saw his kids and grandchildren." But it was always on his terms: "I'll be there at one o'clock," he would say. "And I'll stay for an hour." When they visited his home, the grandkids never slept over. "That's the way he was," says Dan.

Peritz continued to play golf all his life—and he played it well, shooting his age on tough courses even into his eighties. He loved opera ("And made us kids go," Dan says).

Peritz read voraciously, and followed current affairs avidly. Originally a conservative, he moderated his views. He told Dan, "Your mother was active very early about Vietnam. And she was right." As for Donald Trump: "This is not who we are," Peritz said simply.

⚜

Peritz dealt with aging well, Dan says. In his fifties, he began eating less. He went from a robust, former bodybuilder's physique, to a lighter, leaner look. He was always very healthy, but now he looked very good. ("After losing his hair in high school," Dan laughs.)

When Peritz's mother developed Alzheimer's, he and Dan had a few discussions about life and death. "Nothing heavy," Dan says. But his father had become interested in Exit International. The global organization advocates for a person's right to determine the time and manner of their death. Peritz was worried that, like his mother, he was at risk for Alzheimer's. He was, as usual, thinking things through, navigating life on his terms.

Sometime in 2017, Dan noticed that his father was a little less sharp than usual. But his father was active—he continued to drive from his home in White Plains to visit children and grandchildren—and after all, he was nearing his ninth decade.

On April 30, 2018, Dan threw a party at his Westport home. It was Peritz's ninetieth birthday. Surrounded by relatives and friends, celebrating one more milestone in his long life, Peritz had a great time. So did all the guests.

But soon—very quickly—he got very sick. He ate less. He passed out once or twice. He went for tests. The verdict: prostate cancer. It had spread too far to treat.

The siblings talked. Jon suggested an assisted living/skilled nursing facility. They found a great place in Greenwich.

Peritz did not want to go. "That's no life," he said.

So Dan invited his father to live with him in his Westport home.

In late May, less than a month after his diagnosis, Peritz moved in.

Physically, the setup was ideal. Peritz had his own room on the first floor. It faced Gray's Creek, the magnificent inlet ringed with marshes and wildlife just a few yards from Long Island Sound. Dan's room was up on the second floor.

The first morning—and every morning for nearly three months—Peritz got up. He put on a jacket and tie, just as he'd done all his life. But now, instead of going to work, he got in Dan's car. Together with Luke, Dan's labradoodle, they drove around town.

The trio soon established a morning routine. They'd head to Elvira's, the small deli less than a mile away at Old Mill Beach. Peritz would get out of the car, walk inside, and order a muffin. Stacey and Nicky, the energetic, loving, mother-and-daughter owners, would say, "Give him rice pudding!" They doted on him. In turn, he often complimented the women—and everyone else in the deli—on how hard they worked.

When Peritz's energy flagged, he'd tell Dan, "You go in. I'll guard the car." Dan would bring his breakfast back to him.

Inside the deli or not, Peritz was still in psychiatrist/observation mode. He'd watch how people looked, walked, interacted. He'd notice what had changed from the day before, and what had not. He continued to take an active interest in everything going on, everywhere.

Dan, Peritz, and Luke would then drive through Longshore Club Park. They'd make their way slowly through the golf course, past the Inn and the marina, and out the exit road. (Dan's house lies right across the creek). Not much got past Peritz. Once, he noted, "Those guys on the third hole need to work a bit harder."

As Dan drove, his father told stories. He'd remember an old golf partner from the Berkshires, or his daughter's wedding that took place at Pearl of Longshore Club Park. On their morning drive, they would always pass by the Minuteman Press. His dad would say to no one in particular, "Give me liberty or give me death." At the time, Dan didn't connect it to his father's condition, but he does now. Peritz didn't want to live if he couldn't be free.

6

Sometimes, his memories were spontaneous. Other times, Dan would prompt him. "Tell me about the cigar factory," he'd say. Or "I always wondered about . . ."

Left to right: Peritz Levinson, Joye Whitney, Luke (dog), and Dan Levinson on their daily morning drive around Westport, CT (2018).

The conversations were "deep, personal, and funny," Dan says. "My dad was always a minimalist. He didn't become a different person when he got sick. But there was an ease about that time—especially the drives. We didn't have dramatic conversations. They were never boring—always going deeper with more time and openness than in the past. But we'd talk. That was a special time of day."

One morning, a golf ball bounced too close for comfort, directly in front of the car. Dan calls it "one more shared experience." He pauses. "We both raised our eyebrows and looked at each other. I can't describe it—but it was a completely natural, shared experience.

"It was such a pleasure being with him on those drives. He was so appreciative."

When Peritz moved in, Dan considered finding him a trainer at the YMCA. His condition deteriorated too rapidly for that. But Dan was always thinking of ways to keep his father active and involved.

One day, he asked Peritz if he wanted to see the Westport Senior Center—the popular, always-humming building not far from Dan's home.

"Why?" Peritz asked.

But a month later, an opera singer performed there. Dan took his father. He loved it. He returned several times thereafter. Executive Director Sue Pfister got to know Peritz. She'd compliment him on how well he was dressed (particularly, Dan laughs, "compared to his son!"). The Westport Library became another favorite spot. Like Sue, Director Bill Harmer quickly became a Peritz Levinson fan.

As the weeks went on, Dan began jotting down activities they did, emotions he felt, things his father said. He did not want to forget any of them. One line stands out. Not long before he died, Peritz told Dan, "Come outside. It's raining down sunshine!"

Dan and Peritz did not share those final months alone. They had plenty of company. And that made all the difference in the world.

In the beginning, Dan's friends went to Owenoke to "pay respects" to his father. Often, though, that first obligatory visit turned into genuine joy. Thanks to a fortuitous confluence—Peritz's personality, Dan's hospitality, the welcoming floor plan of the waterfront house—the guests got as much out of their visits as Peritz did. Dan's friends returned not because they had to, but because they wanted to. Now they were there not for "Dan's father" but for Peritz himself. He had drawn many new people into his life.

Joye Whitney is a special friend. She and Dan dated for several years. For the first two years, she did not meet Peritz. But she knew of him. "Dan always spoke highly of his dad," Joye says. "I knew all about his intellect, values, dignity, and character."

When they finally met on the front stoop at Dan's second home in Rhode Island, the summer before Peritz got ill, he was "everything I expected," Joye says. "It was his welcoming smile that immediately calmed me. He had an undeniable charm that made conversation easy."

Speaking of him in the present tense, she adds, "He commands his own space. He has presence, due to his stature and the way he holds himself. His overall demeanor and articulation says a lot about who he is. Some of that may be his medical training but it's also who is as an individual, at his core."

When Joye saw him a year later, in Connecticut, she was struck by his physical transformation. He'd lost weight, and was much weaker. But he was still Peritz. And Dan was still—more than ever—Dan.

"It was incredible to watch the father-son bonds," Joye says, of the five weekends she spent that summer in Westport. "I had never witnessed death firsthand in this special way before. I didn't know what to expect, either with our relationship—Dan and I hadn't seen each other in a while—or Peritz's illness."

The first weekend assuaged any fears. When she arrived, Dan's dad was sitting by himself on the front stoop—dressed impeccably— drinking lemonade.

The two of them chatted. He put her at ease. They talked easily, about his day. Later, they listened to music and ate dinner. He loved dessert—and pancakes. "He was so appreciative of everything," she recalls. The weekend "was genuinely fun, not somber," Joye says. "There was so much laughter. For someone ninety and dying, he had more energy than most people."

Still, Joye notes, Peritz was "a different person than before. He knew he was dying. A piece of him had already let go. He was less rigid. There was an ease, a comfort, in who he was." She noticed a similar transformation in Dan.

That first night, as Dan made dinner, he snapped his fingers to music. His father recognized that Dan was happy and nicknamed him "the finger snapper." "That was a real father-son moment," she smiles.

Over the five weekends, Joye got to know Peritz in "a special way." She was one of the few passengers allowed to join their daily drives. Sitting in the back seat next to the dog, Joye watched, fascinated, through the rearview mirror. She saw the father and son as they interacted. She observed their looks, heard their laughter. She felt privileged to be part of their journey.

Dan called his father Pops. The grandchildren called him Ampa. On that initial drive, Joye asked how she should address him.

"Call me anything you want," he replied. "Pops, Ampa . . . my name is Peritz."

On that first drive also—while his son was in Elvira's, getting coffee—Peritz told Joye, "Dan is one of my greatest accomplishments."

"You created a masterpiece," she told him.

"Well, I wouldn't go that far," he joked.

❧

Dan was juggling his obligations to his father and his friend. Peritz came first—and that was fine with Joye.

Dan always called his father "the master of one-liners." Joye remembers one. As the house filled with Dan's friends, Peritz excused himself—"politely, of course"—to go to bed. Dan kept bringing people in to check on him. His father looked up and said, "This is like a museum. You should charge admission."

Each weekend was wonderful, Joye says. Once, Peritz trusted Joye to take Dan shopping for corduroy pants. Peritz wore them often, and wanted Dan to have them too. That meant a lot to her.

Dan says that Joye had "a total crush" on Peritz. His father reciprocated. "He fell for her," Dan says. "He'd ask, 'Is Joye coming this weekend? I want to take her out for a drink.' " Dan thought his dad would be a great wing-man, but he turned out to be competition! Everyone fell for him . . .

Peritz never complained about being sick—not even when he slowed down, his appetite waned, and he felt weak. He was never much of a drinker. But Dan introduced his father to the "five o'clock social drink." He liked the ritual immensely.

The last time Joye visited, they went to Pearl at Longshore. He wanted a drink (and French fries). As they sat on the back deck, a wedding began on the lawn. Peritz told one of his favorite stories: the one about his daughter's wedding.

Then—"So gentlemanly," Joye says—he insisted on paying the bill. He held up his billfold for the waiter.

The waiter took it. But there was nothing inside. Peritz no longer had a need for cash or credit cards.

"That was so stoic, so real, so much about his values of wanting to do what's right," Joye says.

❧

Maristela Payer first met Peritz more than a decade ago, through mutual friends at Brae Burn Country Club in Purchase, New York. She was a Realtor. When he was moving to White Plains, he listed his house in Greenwich with her.

They became close. "He didn't do email," Maristela says. "Everything—all the documents, you name it—was done in person. He really trusted me."

In April 2018, she was invited to Peritz's ninetieth birthday party. She noticed he'd lost weight. A couple of weeks later, Dan called. His father needed assisted living help, Dan said, but insisted he would not make any decisions without his "advisor" Maristela.

Peritz—who did not know that Dan had already spoken with her— also phoned, and asked Maristela to help. She said she'd never searched for anything like that for a client, but would do what she could. When they met, she was struck by how "vulnerable and frail" Peritz looked.

They talked about finding someplace in Greenwich, within walking distance to a coffee shop and the train station. Assisted living facilities require medical exams; she took him for tests.

That's when Dan said he'd bring his father to Westport.

"It all happened so naturally," Maristela remembers. "He felt comfortable with Dan. It was beautiful to see the dance between them. They were not just father and son. They became best friends."

She first visited in early July. Over the next few weeks, she watched him grow happier and happier in his new home. Little things—Dan's dog sleeping on the floor next to him, the five o'clock "happy hour" with drinks, salad, and ice cream—meant so much to him.

Despite Peritz's prognosis, he remained optimistic. One afternoon, he and Maristela made plans to go to Florida in the winter—or perhaps Central America. "He looked ahead to more days and months of good life," she says.

The last time they visited, Peritz told Maristela that he did not feel well. However, he said, the love he had received from Dan, and Dan's children, meant so much to him. When she left, he was happy and joking.

"I'm from South America," Maristela says. "We take care of people. We don't send them to nursing homes. What Dan did was rare here. And the fact that he became his father's best friend, that's rare, too."

Peritz looked forward to each visit. "Who's coming today?" he would ask Dan.

He took pleasure in every visitor. One day, concerned he needed a haircut before a visitor arrived, Peritz wondered, "Where can a fellow get shined up around here?"

Dan brought Mr. Joseph—a hairstylist—to the house. Peritz was pleased. Then he had a manicure. He loved that too.

The last time Joye saw Peritz was two weeks before he died. Peritz had fallen, and Dan told her not to come to Connecticut. It was a stressful time; Dan was not sleeping. But Peritz was well cared for, by his son and a team of nurses.

"It was incredible to watch up to that point," Joye says. "His departure seemed to be pain-free. He was so dignified. And he was at home, surrounded by the people he loved most."

Joye and Peritz are both early risers. They often sat outside together, watching the Owenoke ospreys.

On her final weekend with Peritz, they did not see the magnificent raptors. Now, on visits to Dan, she sees them often. She calls them "a spiritual reminder" of Peritz.

She feels sad that she never got to say goodbye. But she recalls their final conversation well. Joye asked Peritz, "What should I know about Dan? We've only been friends for a few years—not a lifetime."

"He needs somebody to work *with* him," Dan's father said.

"I'll never forget that," Joye says. "It seems so simple. But it resonated with me."

While growing up, Dan's son Jesse saw his grandfather often, and he admired his brilliance. One day, Jesse asked a question about Sigmund Freud. To his grandson's amusement (and eventual impatience), Peritz spent two hours answering.

Jesse did share Peritz's last months with him. The summer after his freshman year in college he worked as a counselor at Earthplace, ran a window-washing company whimsically called Suds Studs, and spent what little free time he had at Dan's house, coming and going at all hours of the day and night with his room next to his grandfather's.

Clockwise from top left: Jesse Levinson, Adam Levinson, Steve Ferriera (grandson-in-law), Hayley Kahn, Peritz Levinson, and Andie Levinson, at his son Dan's Westport, CT home (2018).

Like Dan's friends—who came over first to see Dan's father, then returned to "visit Peritz"—the teenager's buddies enjoyed interacting with his grandfather. "He acted like he'd always known my friends," Jesse says.

Jesse's sister Andie works at Sotheby's and lives in New York City. She was a bit surprised when her father brought Peritz into his home.

"My dad definitely likes his space," she says, but she adds admiringly, "He's never better than in an emergency, or when someone needs help."

She and her brother Adam—who works in venture capital, and also lives in New York—took the train to Westport on several summer weekends. Her grandfather "loved hearing about my week, and what I was doing. He felt involved."

Andie has strong memories of Peritz before he became sick. When she got engaged, she very much wanted him at a special party. He was at his Florida home, and no one expected him to come. But she printed out a Paperless Post invitation and mailed it to him—he did not use a computer—and sure enough, he showed up.

In fact, he arrived early. He had a great time, and stayed late. Andie appreciates that party even more now, because Peritz won't be at her wedding.

Her grandfather was always "a settled person," Andie says. In his final months, he became even more centered. "He was happy to sit on the couch with us, just as if he wasn't sick." She particularly enjoyed watching his connection with Dan's dog. "Ampa couldn't turn his head without Luke watching him and trying to help," Andie says.

Peritz was around nearly every weekend until Adam was ten, Andie's brother recalls. "He did a loop on Sunday, to visit the siblings and cousins. I'm sure years from now, my dad will do the same thing."

Peritz was "like any grandfather. He'd sit on the carpet, and we built blocks." Adam saw less of him in later years. But, "He was always great: a soft person, very insightful, and a fantastic listener." In twenty-five years, Adam never saw his grandfather get mad.

Peritz was "the essence of class. He was not fancy; he was 'couth.' When I'd do boy stuff, he'd say, 'That's uncouth, Adam.' He set a great example for me, as a respectful adult."

When Peritz got sick, Adam appreciated the chance to visit him in Westport. However, he notes, "There was never an expectation I'd come each weekend, or have long, deep conversations." They talked of basic, here-and-now things: Adam's job, or the vegetables in the garden.

When Peritz died, Adam was realistic. "He was ninety. He'd lived a great life. I was almost thinking more of my dad. I couldn't imagine losing him. I thought about how nice it was that he and his father had that time together."

Peritz's death "wasn't sudden or ugly. It was beautiful. That took a lot of the sadness out of it. People do get old. They die. This seems like a good way to do it."

Years from now, Adam says, he hopes that he and his siblings can do for their father the same thing he did for his.

Peritz Levinson with son Jonathan Levinson (1963).

Jesse, Andie and Adam were not the only relatives who shared in Peritz's final months. Dan's brother Jon was very close to his father. "Everything I did was made possible by Jon," Dan says. "He runs a cool business, and lives in New York City with his special needs son, who he's eternally devoted to. Still, he came every weekend to sit and visit, as he and my dad had done for years."

Jon took care of much of the administrative and financial paperwork during Peritz's illness. He also handled many medical questions. "He took big, complex issues off the shoulders of the rest of us—and always with a cheery, can-do attitude," Dan notes. "I was lucky to have him as a partner."

Peritz with his children. From left to right: Dan Levinson, Deb Weber, Peritz Levinson, and Jonathan Levinson (2006).

Their sister Deb has five children. One has a serious illness, and underwent a crisis during Peritz's final months. She gave all that she could to her father and brothers. They are grateful for her love and support.

Gwen Tutun met Dan when they lived in the same New York City apartment building. Later, both moved to Westport. She met Peritz after he moved in with Dan. Like so many people, her first visit led to more.

"He struck me as extremely brilliant, academic, and courtly. He wore a jacket with a pocket square," she recalls. "He was the kind of gentleman you don't see now."

No matter how much discomfort he was in, "He always seemed interested in other people. We sat and talked about our lives and ideas. He was always so present. It was so enjoyable, just sitting and talking."

During the summer, Dan hosted a political fundraiser. His father had lost a great deal of weight and looked ill. However, Gwen says, "He still offered his seat to a woman and stood." Two days later, he died.

Eileen Lavigne Flug and Dan have been partners in a number of local initiatives. She first met Peritz when she went to Dan's house to borrow a kayak. As with so many others, Peritz's personality pulled her into his orbit. She visited half a dozen times more.

Once, he volunteered to teach her to play bridge. They sat at the kitchen table and had a great afternoon. "I never got to have a second lesson," she says wistfully.

A decade ago, Monique Bosch and Dan helped start the Green Village Initiative, Westport's non-profit environmental organization. She met Peritz a few times before he got sick.

When he moved into Dan's house, she says, he was even more calm and optimistic than before. "He was almost child-like," she says. Small things made him happy, Monique noticed, like cherries from the garden.

"He was fun and funny to the end. He made all of us feel so welcome. He said he was glad to see us. He wanted everyone to feel good."

Watching her friend take care of his father that summer, Monique gained insights into both men. "I saw Dan's pureness and goodness," she says. "And I saw it in his dad, too. It was such a beautiful thing to watch and be part of."

The night Peritz died—as he lay in bed, in some pain—Monique came by. "Hi!" she said. "I just came to see you. Maybe I'll come back later."

"No," he joked. "As you can see, I've made a full recovery."

As Peritz's condition deteriorated, Dan had become even more watchful and attentive.

Doctors warned the cancer might spread to his brain. One night, Peritz repeated the phrase "two up, three down" over and over. Dan asked what it meant.

"If I knew, I wouldn't say it!" his father replied.

Hospice care began in mid-August.

That experience was "amazing," Dan says. "They showed up all the time. They were very kind, caring and practical." They took care of all the details, including pain medication, so Dan and his family—and Peritz—could concentrate on saying goodbye. Peritz appreciated that these were "real people" coming into his home and not a sterile hospital. He valued their practical experience and knowledge.

Dan later recalled, "When I was little, I went with him to open and close our cottage. It was always my honor to work next to him. During these final weeks, when we were alone in the house and I was doing something, Pops would say, 'Need any help, Dan?' This felt like a reversal of roles." But there was such a sweetness and connection in it.

During Peritz's final hours, Dan got into bed next to his father. Even though he theoretically couldn't speak or move, his father out of the blue said clear as day, "Got enough room, Dan?" Always caring for his family first.

Finally, Dan gave his father morphine. Peritz relaxed. The nurse went in another room. Dan put an opera on the speakers. He lowered the lights, lit a few candles, and opened the windows so Peritz's spirit could soar.

His breathing slowed. Then it stopped. Luke, the dog, was with Peritz on the bed.

Since Peritz died, Joye says, she has become "more accepting of death. I'm not afraid of it, no matter how it unfolds. It can be an amazing gift."

She has learned, too, "the value of time. Five weeks was not enough time to have with Peritz. But I'm very lucky to have had them."

Thanks to Peritz, Joye has found "a whole new way of looking at Dan."

Maristela, too, never imagined she would grow so close to Peritz. The summer she spent as he lived and died made her "appreciate every minute I have life. Today, I do my best to be in touch with the people I love. You never know . . ."

A year later, she says, "I think about him, and miss him. I look at his picture and smile. He was a dear friend. He made such an impact on me."

He made an impact on Eileen, too. She is grateful she could see the "wonderful experience" of Peritz being in a warm, loving home. "He glided through the rooms. He was smiling, happy, peaceful. He had his son, a beautiful view of the water, his grandchildren—that was all he needed. I'll never forget that."

Monique has spent time as a hospice volunteer. She has seen death close up. But, she says, "I never saw anyone with as much spunk as Peritz. He was unique. As a psychiatrist, he may have even looked forward to the adventure. What was on the other side?"

Spending the summer with his father and grandfather showed Jesse what it means to care for someone you love—and made him think about his future as well.

Jesse's sister Andie says, "If I could choose how I could go, I'd do it the exact way he did. At ninety, after a great life, he was watching all his children and grandchildren, in not too much pain, in one of his children's home. There's a lot of grace and beauty in that."

She thinks that things happen for a reason. In mid-August, she was supposed to head to Florida with her fiance's family. "Peritz couldn't wrap his head around why anyone would want to go to Florida in the summer," she says.

"He died hours before I was supposed to get on the plane. There's absolutely a piece of me that believes he died when he did—well, the timing was elegant. And he was, too."

After Dan's mother died of lung cancer, he spent several months "wandering around." It took him a year to feel "normal."

"With Pops, it was not the same," he says. He misses his "best friend," yet knows he could not feel sad. "He'd never want that," Dan knows.

Dan recognizes that his circumstances were, if not unique, then certainly out of the ordinary.

He had a large, lovely house, big enough to accommodate his dad, and situated beautifully enough to offer peace and serenity. Though relatively young, Dan was already semi-retired. His three children were all out of high school.

"If I had three little kids and was barely paying my mortgage, I know I couldn't have done this," he says. "Most people are under constant pressure just to survive. My brother and sister loved our dad as much as I do. But they have families and work. Both have special needs sons.

"I'm happy and grateful I could do this. It was the chance of a lifetime. A total honor."

Dan thought of a phrase he'd heard from Great Plains Native American culture. "It's a good day to die," older people would say.

Dan thought his father had a similar spirit. "He was an elegant, low-maintenance, very present man. He was very conscious of his death. He never said, 'I'm afraid to die.' His slate was clean. He had no unfinished business with anyone. He was as happy as he ever was. He had a beautiful life, and a wonderful way to go. His death was a gift to me." When he first walked in this house to stay, he announced, "I've been low-maintenance my whole life, and we're not gonna change that now . . ."

Dan notes, "For millions of years, human beings lived in small groups. When someone got sick, everyone took care of them. The last two hundred years, society has gotten away from that. I'm so lucky I had the chance that so many people today don't get."

Dan knows, too, that his father's final days were as good as they could be. "He never got angry. He never got messy. I know that's not always the case.

"I thought it would be hard," Dan says. "It wasn't."

He stops and looks out at the water.

"I'd do it again tomorrow."

Nancy Kuhn-Clark at Armonk, NY (1990).

Lucky at Love
• Nancy Kuhn-Clark •

by Sheryl Kayne

March 2, 2016

"I WAS DIAGNOSED WITH ALS [Amyotrophic Lateral Sclerosis, a fatal neurodegenerative disease] when I was sixty," Nancy shared her story with Dr. Huned Patwa's class at the Yale School of Medicine.

"Sitting in this wheelchair, the irony that strikes me is that before ALS, I never sat still in my life. The other irony is how incredibly lucky I've always been. Lucky at love, lucky in Las Vegas. ALS does not define me. I am still me: thankful, joyous, and appreciative, loving living every day.

"One of my major hopes for the future is that young people like you will find answers where there aren't any yet. It is unfathomable that in 1969 we put a man on the moon, yet since 1939, when Lou Gehrig [first baseman for the New York Yankees] was diagnosed, we still haven't been able to figure out how to fix dying motor neurons. You can change that.

"People are always telling me, 'Oh, you are so brave.' I don't feel brave at all. This happened to me. This is the situation. I must live with the hand I was dealt and will keep doing that as long as possible."

The Diagnosis

"Our son Elliot was studying abroad for a semester in Vienna, fall 2010.

Bob and I visited him and traveled around Europe. This was our first major awareness of my earliest symptoms: trouble walking and fatigue. The Duomo in Florence, Italy has four hundred fifty steps. It was not easy for me to make it to the top or to be a real tourist in a walking city. Throughout 2011, I went into the 'I must-be-fat and middle-aged and need to get into shape' mode by joining the YMCA, swimming, and watching what I ate.

"No improvement, but not really worse, except that I felt twitches in my thighs and severe cramping in my toes. I knew something was wrong and tried acupuncture and physical therapy; however, we weren't sure what we were treating.

"Bob and I began serious medical investigation in March 2012, which took loads of doctors and tests over a year and a half. The confirmed medical diagnosis came from Dr. Patwa in October 2013, but my husband and I guessed it was ALS before anyone else.

"Having Dr. Patwa's confirmation was devastating, yet a relief to know we were all in agreement what it was."

Bob clearly remembers the day, time, and place. "We were in Ogunquit, Maine, summer 2013. After months and months of going to doctors and more doctors, Nancy was searching and researching on her own. She asked me to sit down, held my hand, and said, 'I know what's wrong with me. It's ALS.'

"Honestly, I was totally in denial up to that point," says Bob, "positive there would be a fixable solution. But she was so meticulous with her research, it all became very real to me."

Every step of the way, on her own or with a cane, walker, or wheelchair, Nancy refused to stop doing what she had always done: maintaining her life, putting her family and friends first, providing everyone with the person she truly was and that they knew and loved. She lived each day going forward as she had lived each day past, with thankfulness, joy, spark, thoughtfulness, and kindness.

Nancy always woke up with a huge smile. There was never any looking back or woe. She greeted each day with enthusiasm—excited to shower, dress, and take that first sip of coffee. She had a sweet tooth and especially loved Neuhaus chocolates and her daughter Emily's brownies. The only thing she wanted to eat at the end of her life was Emily's brownie sundaes. Most importantly, she was determined and committed to be the mother, wife, sister, friend, and person she always was, despite the disease wracking her body.

"There was only one dark cloud for Nancy," says Bob, "one thing I could not fix for her when she told me, 'The only regret I have is that I will never meet my grandchildren. I can deal with everything else.' "

Armed with the confirmed diagnosis, Nancy's priority was to pave the way for her children to continue living healthy lives, pursuing their goals, being strong and productive without her. And they are.

Constance is working towards her PhD in Educational Public Policy at Columbia University in New York. Emily recently graduated with her master's degree in Public Policy from the Lyndon B. Johnson School of Public Affairs at the University of Texas. She moved to DC, where she worked a fellowship/apprenticeship on Capitol Hill for Representative Joaquin Castro by day and completed her remaining classes at night. Elliot works in publishing in New York City.

Gifts and Love Letters

"She left each of us with a very personal note to be opened after she died," says Constance. "She actually began writing them when she was first diagnosed. You can see, she'd leave and come back to them, intentionally adding in motherly advice and things to remember that we shared. She teased me about my huge interest in yoga and ordered a sculpture from India, a mother holding her child. They are connected into infinity, to always remind me of us. We will always be connected.

"Growing up, I loved dressing up and acting out the parts in *Mary Poppins* and *West Side Story*, including the accents. Her last letter to me referred to that time in our lives, how what she loved about me was how uninhibited and fresh and fun life can be. She didn't want me to ever lose sight of that. Mom encouraged me to find happiness in my life beyond my PhD. Probably the most important line in her note said, 'Have fun and allow yourself to eat peppermint ice cream whenever you want to.'

"She had no concern about what the future of her ALS would be like for her," says Constance, "but wanted to make sure that we were prepared to handle what was coming. It's been almost two years since she died and it still feels remarkably fresh and new. She left me a pearl necklace I loved playing with, whenever she held me in her arms when I was very young. Now, I wear it all of the time."

Nancy's younger daughter, Emily, had similar recollections as her older sister. "In true Mom form," says Emily, "she shared her memories of me as a child, the things she admired about me, the advice she wanted me to have, remember, and cherish.

"I will always treasure the experience Mom and I shared getting my dog, Lucy. I asked for a dog every birthday, Christmas, you name it, but Dad is allergic and my parents always said no. I loved dachshunds; my mom did, too. One of my high school classmate's fathers owned a pet store, and a litter of miniature dachshunds were arriving. I begged Mom to go see them. 'Just to look!' I promised.

"Two mini-dachshunds were in a playpen. The boy doggie ran all around, nibbling and playing with anything he could find. Lucy sat in the corner, nervously shaking. Mom whispered, 'Grab her.' I scooped her right up, she licked us both, and we fell in love. Mom said almost instantly, 'Okay. We will just get her.' I was shocked. My mother never made impulsive decisions or purchases. She did not shop and never bought anything big for herself. Something about Lucy, along with something about me with Lucy, spoke to her. It was the most impulsive decision I ever saw her make. She grew to really love Lucy. We called her 'Mom's little therapy dog.' At night, when I showered, Lucy laid across the bed on Mom's legs until I came out."

Emily's twin brother, Elliot, has his own favorite memories. "Because Mom is so old-fashioned and loved books," says Elliot, "she gave me an atlas to encourage me to continue traveling and think of her. She wrote in my message, 'Try not to overthink. Don't be afraid to make the wrong decision. Most decisions aren't life-altering anyway, and it's not worth the time spent or the stress.' Best of all, she told me to remember what she always used to say. 'The things we spend time worrying about don't usually come to pass. And things we never saw coming wind up biting us in the ass!' "

Mom to Many Children

Beverly and Nancy in Fairfield, CT (2015).

"All Nancy ever really wanted was to be happily married and a mom. Her earliest mother-in-training began when I was born," says her sister Beverly (Nancy is also survived by another sister, Susan, and their mother, Margarete). "Susan was thirteen months old when Nancy was born, but Nancy was nine and a half when I arrived. Nancy literally raised me, taking it upon herself to fill the mom role. The family story goes that whenever Nancy took me out for a walk in the baby carriage, she'd tell anyone who stopped, 'Don't touch the baby! You can look at the baby, but don't touch.'

"We grew up in Great Neck, New York. Nancy made everything easier for me and brought me along with her on her life journey. There was always joy, fun, excitement, and love. When she was in high school, dating the ever-so-cool and popular greaser—think John Travolta and Olivia Newton John long before the movie was made—I was part of the deal, going everywhere they did.

"She taught me all about her many jobs as a flower truck delivery driver, a florist, and then creating the floral arrangements. I rode on the truck with her and could name every flower and plant as well as how to care for them.

"Nancy was one of the most intelligent people I ever met. She could process, understand, and strip things down to what really mattered. Emotional in love but not thought, her reasoning capacity was unparalleled. Her kindness was genuine, and her interaction with others was honest and authentic. Nancy taught me about every aspect of life and, ultimately, about death."

When asked by Yale students about her religion or faith, Nancy responded, "I am not religious, so my faith is in people. I honestly don't know what I would do without Bob. He has loved me and been there for me every step of the way. We still have candlelit dinners almost every night.

"My sister, Beverly, is a saint, living about forty-five minutes to an hour away; she spends one to three days a week with me. She insists that I make a to-do list: sew a button, untangle a necklace, go on an outing, organize a drawer or a closet, or hang out and watch a movie, so Bob can go out without fear of leaving me alone. Friends are always checking in on me, too, sharing so much thoughtfulness and kindness— a lunch or supper (our meals on wheels), a bunch of flowers, a book, or my Dammit Doll for stress relief."

Surrounded by Books

"Nancy loved the Westport Library so much, if I set up a bed for her, she would have loved living there," says Bob. "She would have worked there even if she wasn't being paid. You don't very often meet people who turn a task into a labor of love."

Nancy earned a bachelor's degree in English and then a master's in education at New York University (NYU). She worked as an English substitute teacher in Great Neck and then grades six, seven, and eight at Roslyn Middle School. Later, she applied for and accepted a job at *The Village Voice*, where her future husband, Bob, hired her for a job she had never done before and was her boss. Nancy said it best: "Eventually we were married, and then I became the boss."

When Constance, Emily, and Elliot were young, Nancy worked part-time in the children's library and enjoyed it so much that she went back to school for a second master's degree in library science. Years passed, the kids grew, and her part-time job became full time. She worked her way into the reference department once she completed her degree.

"One thing I will never forget is that after I was diagnosed," Nancy shared with Dr. Patwa's class, "a new and exciting position was created at the library, Manager of Learning and Discovery. Under normal circumstances, that was my dream job, and I would have applied; however, I knew it would require a lot of energy, supervising quite a few other departments, and meeting multiple strategic goals. So, I let it go. I was walking with a cane and was unsure if I could keep up the pace.

"About a month later, the library director, Maxine Bleiweiss, asked to see me. We talked about my condition briefly and carefully. I thought maybe there was a little unspoken HIPPA [Health Insurance Portability and Accountability Act of 1996 protects and assures privacy of medical information] anxiety in the room, because she was generally a straight shooter. She wondered if I had made any plans.

"I told her, 'I truthfully do not know how much longer I can work, but certainly I am not ready to stop. I would like to stay as long as I am earning my paycheck.'

From left: Elliot, Bob, Constance, Nancy, and Emily at Ogunquit, Maine (circa 1992).

"She nodded and leaned in a little and asked what I thought about taking the Learning and Discovery position on an interim basis, or as long as we agreed it made sense. The next thing I remember is very unprofessionally tearing up, nodding my head, and whispering, 'Wow!' That was the capstone to my career."

Maxine remembers every detail. "Looking back at that time," says Maxine, "I advertised for applicants, but Nancy was perfect. She became the head of our new department, Learning and Discovery, in September 2014. We made bathroom accommodations for her and, otherwise, the building was new enough to be wheelchair accessible. I knew she would know when she was ready to leave."

That trust and faith meant a great deal to Nancy. "Maxine's putting faith in me and promoting me under those circumstances spoke volumes about her. I worked my hardest to exceed all expectations. I was always running, always on the go. Eventually, the cane gave way to a walker, which gave way to a manual wheelchair, which gave way to a motorized wheelchair. I worked at the Westport Library for seventeen years and stopped working July 2015, just a few weeks following Maxine's retirement."

New Job, New Friends

"Nancy and I met in December 2014," says Robin Powell, the Executive Administrative Assistant to the Director of the Westport Library. "We became fast friends. I just loved her from the moment we met, and the feeling was mutual.

"I began noticing changes in her and one day just asked, 'I noticed there's a change in you, are you okay?'

" 'No, I'm not okay,' she said in the lovely way she always spoke. 'I'm going to die. I have ALS.'

"My new, wonderful friend and I never did anything together when she wasn't sick. Dying became the foundation of our friendship. If I intended to help her die gracefully, she told me, 'Treat me normally. Just go about your business as you ordinarily would.'

"I asked if it was okay to ask, 'How are you feeling?'

" 'Yes.'

" 'How are you feeling?'

"She responded, 'It sucks.'

"It was an emotional ride, meeting someone so wonderful, instantly bonding, and learning she was dying and watching her decline. I can still hear her lovely voice. Her absence of grumbling or complaining changed me. She taught me grace, humility, and patience. She blessed me by being my friend for the short time we had.

"When she started to slow way down, she retired. I visited her at home to chat and brought her lobster chowder, which she loved. Food and eating were a big part of our relationship. When she could no longer eat, I brought flowers.

"She never once complained. Just before Christmas 2015, I arrived home to find a big box waiting for me with a stunning bay leaf wreath inside without a note. I snapped a photo and posted it on Facebook. 'Look, I have a Secret Santa!' She sent me gifts for Mother's Day and my birthday. She cared so much about me and my children and other people's lives. I've never known anyone else like her. I saw this incredible person who didn't change between work and her way of being away from work. Because she was so passionate about what she did, she never went into nonwork mode. She carried that joy of learning and discovering because that was her, a person who made it possible for all the people around her to do the same."

Like Robin, Deborah White met Nancy at the Westport Library. They began working in the children's department at the same time. In 2013, they found that they were both experiencing similar symptoms and were undergoing extensive testing at the same time. "We compared notes and test results. In a way, it made the process easier," says Deborah.

It turned out that one disease was manageable, and one was not. "The day we discovered our diagnoses still plays over and over in my mind." Deborah pauses to wipe away a tear. "Two friends walking down a path as it split into two directions. That was one of the worst days of my life.

"The best is that she was my friend. She taught me that it's okay not to have anything to say. Sometimes, it is just being present."

Mom's Focus Was Us; Our Focus Was Her

"The call from Mom and Dad telling me that this was ALS and we must battle this together," says Elliot, "was a call to action. We all knew the prognosis. In 2015, I transferred from working in Atlanta to New York so that I could be in Connecticut almost every weekend. My sisters were also in Manhattan and Brooklyn. Constance and I were always texting, calling, visiting on weekends, and meeting with Mom on Facetime. Emily became the primary caretaker, fully in charge and making the tough decisions daily.

"I usually arrived on Friday night or Saturday morning. We went wherever Mom wanted to go, to the beach or Costco, looking for deals. We spent so much time over the last few years together that we bonded as adults. It was so great having that time with her right up to the very end. I'm fortunate I had the foresight and the maturity from growing up with her that everything else in my life could wait. There were many good times from 2014 to 2017. The final six to twelve months were really difficult, but I asked her everything I wanted to know, to have her confirmation of what life was all about and what she wanted for me. Mom gave me the gift of her, and I'll never forget a minute of it.

"She taught me how to make linzer torte in exactly the same way her father and grandfather traditionally did. (I reminded her of her dad, Henry, which is my middle name.) She gave me all of the tools we used to mold the dough and put it all together with currant, raspberry, and apricot preserves. I cherish her handwritten recipes with the neat and perfect handwriting. She was the perfectionist baker, Dad was the gourmet cook. It was a great combination."

Bob and Nancy in Ogunquit, Maine (circa 1990).

Working Together: Accepting Support

Emily moved home in July 2017 to take care of Nancy. Her degree was in government studies from Georgetown University. She wanted to return to DC and get a master's degree, but "I put it all on hold and went home to be with my mom," says Emily. "Initially, we thought I would regroup and study for the GREs and apply to master's programs while spending time with her; however, her condition deteriorated in a way that I was not privy to before actually moving in. I'm not sure if my parents knew this, or if they simply weren't ready to face it or to tell me. It became clear quickly that my father was no longer able to take care of her, that we did not have private care, and that they needed much more than any of us realized.

From left: Bob, Nancy, Emily, Constance, and Elliot at Emily's graduation from Georgetown (circa 2009).

"The most special activity that my mom and I shared was our love for the *New York Times* Sunday crossword puzzle. It arrived in the NYT magazine on Saturdays with the weekend paper, and we worked on it all week. She was smart and had such an amazing gift for words and language. After moving home, I sat in bed with her after she was changed and teeth brushed. She would put her oxygen mask on, even after an exhausting day with all the energy it took just to breathe and live her life; she looked at the puzzle, pointed to the clue, and dictated her answer, which was always right. This underscored how unbelievably terrible this disease was for her. She was more than all there mentally, yet she couldn't hold the magazine, let alone write in the words, but she still carried the team! Now, I have the NYT crossword app on my phone and do it myself each night in bed. I am terrible at it without her. I haven't even come close to finishing one since she died.

"My mom's favorite thing that I did for her was returning home. She was overwhelmed by what I became—her advocate and caretaker. I know she was impressed and proud of how capable I turned out to be in the situation, because she kept telling me. It meant everything to her and to me. She viewed this as 'the ultimate act of love and sacrifice.'

"That was sobering for me. Moving home to do this 'job' was the best thing I ever did. I never had the bond built with her with anyone else, except possibly if I have a child. Mom trusted me so completely, she literally put her life in my hands. She was completely dependent on me in every way a person can be. I am okay today because I did not let her down. I gave her all I had and know I did right by her. That helps me keep going.

"In the beginning of my life, she cared for me much the same way I cared for her at the end of hers. The role reversal is baffling, but so sacred. She didn't want anyone else but me to take care of her. We used to joke that she wouldn't even let Dad give her medicine. If anyone else tried helping her, she said, 'Get Emily.'

"I knew what she wanted, what she needed, what she was going to say before she said anything. She didn't need to tell my anything. I just knew her at the purest level, her micro expressions, face and body language. If she didn't like the taste of something, if she had to go to the bathroom, if she wanted to say something or get someone's attention, I knew her on an unspoken, deeply connected way. The bond I had with my mom is so special to me, it erased the teenage angst or early turmoil in our relationship. We would have done anything and everything for each other. And we did. That is love."

The last few days of her life, Nancy said she didn't want to get up. She wasn't doing as well when she was up and out. Emily was on top of it and made the decision to let her stay in bed. Bob, Constance, Emily, Elliot, and Beverly reassured her they would all be okay. Nancy had been preparing for that moment years ahead.

Nancy and Bean's Neighborhood

Bean Corcoran and her family were neighbors down the street from the Clarks when they all lived in Weston. Their children were near the same ages and they played together between the houses.

"Nancy was smart, thoughtful, and compassionate all at the same time and, amazingly, all of the time. We were very close friends for about twenty-eight years," says Bean. "Although we were complete opposites, she was my mentor and best friend. She liked to bake and follow instructions; I like to cook and never follow instructions. She was straight and narrow. I am hippy-ish, always doing my own thing. She wanted everything lined up perfectly; I am loose and laid back.

"We never had an argument, but once she was really mad at me. Emily, then six years old, arrived at my house wiggling at her tooth." Bean pauses dramatically. "I pulled it out. I wasn't supposed to do that. It was Nancy's job and privilege to pull her children's teeth.

"Most often, Nancy told me, 'I really love your beautiful garden.' I put in a few ramps, so that she had another place she could comfortably come to and just hang out. There was a ramp into the front of the house and another from the kitchen into the backyard. I wanted her to always be happy in my home. Our girlfriends, Sarah and Karen, came over with their husbands. It was great fun, four couples all cooking together and enjoying each other.

"Having her memorial service here in our garden/backyard just seemed like the most natural and wonderful thing to do. Her favorite flowers were lilac, sunflowers, zinnias, peonies, and most recently, moonflowers. My husband came up with the idea of planting a lilac tree as part of the memorial service.

"I often find myself looking out at it thriving and growing beautifully. It reminds me of what a kind and wonderful person we had in our lives. I know it's nice for our family and Nancy's to see it here and remember that each person at her memorial service helped plant it in her honor."

In Memoriam

Elliot shared some secrets about Nancy at her memorial service that would have definitely made her laugh out loud.

"Mom had some funny ways. She was very nosy, she liked to know everything, and loved surprising us, but not so much vice versa.

"She always requested that we pour the cream in first, followed by the coffee, and not the other way around. She liked the window blinds open halfway, not all the way, and definitely not closed. She had an excellent sense of smell and was very sensitive to room temperature. She was a neat freak who needed her living space to be pretty and clean at all times. Even in her final weeks, she would signal to me from her chair and whisper through her breathing mask, 'Elliot, honey, there are crumbs on the table.'

"My mom liked nice things but was not materialistic. She cared about value but was not cheap. She was compassionate but also strict and firm. She was just so balanced like that. If you wanted praise from my mom, show her something beautiful and tell her you got it on sale. Or better yet, show her something from nature that is priceless.

"My mom was a librarian and a voracious reader. In her last letter to me, she wrote, 'Life is a book. The fact that it was a short book does not mean it wasn't a good book. It was a very good book.' "

Bob and Nancy at Au Palm, Palm Beach, Florida
(circa 2016).

Author's Note

Many thanks to Nancy's family, friends, and co-workers who all contributed to her story: Robert Clark, Constance Clark, Emily Clark, Elliot Clark, Beverly Kuhn Baynard, Robin Powell, Deborah White, Margie Frielich-Den, Maxine Bleiweiss, Bean Corcoran, and Dr. Huned Patwa.

Reverend Frank Hall in the pulpit, The Unitarian Church of Westport (1990).

In Sickness and in Health
• Frank Hall •

by Frank Hall
& Lory Nurenberg

FRANK

Welcome, O Life. I go to encounter for the millionth time the reality of experience and to forge in the smithy of my soul the uncreated conscience of my race.

—James Joyce, *A Portrait of the Artist as a Young Man*

JAMES JOYCE'S FIRST BOOK WAS a self-portrait; it was a line marking the end of his childhood and the beginning of the great challenge of what lies between birth and life's inevitable conclusion. A favorite passage from Ecclesiastes 3: 1-8 in the Hebrew Bible is attributed to King Solomon. "To everything there is a season, and a time for every purpose under heaven: a time to be born, and a time to die."

Life is what happens between birth and death, and it involves some struggle and some suffering. The struggle and the suffering are teachers; they don't merely provide knowledge or information, but they provide experience that may lead to wisdom. Wisdom is a kind of spirituality, a knowing-ness beyond words; it is poetry, the language of the soul. As a product of intuition, it comes from the heart.

To illustrate, the summer I turned eight, I broke a promise I had made to my mother. It was an implicit promise to stay away from the water. My brother Bill, who was two years older than I, and Bobby McCarthy, who was ten, were exploring in the Medford woods about a mile or so from home.

We discovered two small rafts and tried to float them. When we went home for lunch, my mother noticed my sneakers were wet, so I told her about the rafts. She said, "Keep away from the water." She was emphatic.

I intended to do so. But I was the youngest of the trio. And they wanted to go right back after we ate. I felt conflicted but went along with them.

Two other boys we didn't know showed up. They said that the rafts were made by Boy Scouts, which gave the boys, as well as the rafts, some sense of credibility. The boats were on the edge of what amounted to a big mud puddle about the dimensions of a swimming pool.

One of the rafts was stuck in the mud. Lured by the adventure, I climbed on, using one of the poles that were on the raft and trying to push it out. One of the boys took the other. I was standing on the part of the raft that was floating, while my helper stood on dry ground and gave my raft a strong push.

The push sent me flying through the air, landing in what must have been the deepest part of the water. It was over my head—way over. I couldn't swim.

I have a vivid memory of being in that muddy water and thinking I was going to die. Bill told me later he counted each of the eight times my head bobbed up.

I remember silently protesting, "I'm not supposed to die here—I'm just a kid. I'm not old enough to die now."

Bobby McCarthy bravely jumped in to rescue me. Holding onto the raft with one hand and grabbing my shirt with the other, he pulled me to safety. I was covered with mud from head to toe; Bobby was muddy except for his head and one arm.

We headed home.

This early confrontation with death had a profound and lasting influence on me. I felt (and feel) a very deep sense of appreciation for *not* dying in the Medford woods. After more than seventy years, I carry vivid memories of that day. There's a passage in an E. E. Cummings poem: "i who have died am alive again today, / and this is the sun's birthday."

We human beings are capable of selfless acts that allow a ten-year-old boy to jump into the muddy water to save a friend from drowning.

On my sixtieth birthday, I went back to the neighborhood to look for Bobby, only to discover he had died a few years ago. In my imagination, he says, "What did you do with the life I saved?"

I wanted to tell him. I wanted to thank him. I don't remember ever thanking him. I wanted to acknowledge the ingredient in him that had urged him to save my life.

"Inasmuch as ye have done it unto one of the least of these my brethren, ye have done it to me." (Matthew 25:40 King James Version)

In Hardship and In Ease

Eleven years ago, I was diagnosed with Parkinson's disease.

In December 2007, I had been serving The Unitarian Church in Westport as Senior Minister for twenty-three years. One of the traditions I introduced was an annual reading from Dickens' *A Christmas Carol*. I was sitting on a stool that Sunday morning with my feet resting on the rung near the base of the stool, and my right foot started to shake. I tried to brace my foot against the floor but the shaking didn't stop.

The next day, I called Dr. Altbaum and made an appointment. He gave me a brief exam and told me it could possibly be essential tremor, a relatively benign neurological condition that causes hand shaking when doing tasks. He also suggested it could be Parkinson's disease. He told me to come back in a couple of months, which I did.

During that time between visits, I went into a protective mode. I did notice slight tremors in my fingers while holding my hymnal on Sunday mornings, but I chose to believe my symptoms were caused by essential tremor. I was convinced.

The next exam was more thorough. Dr. Altbaum probed about daily activities like walking, balance, and eating. I commented about my difficulty writing in my journal, noting how small my writing had gotten. He used the word "micrographia" as one of the common symptoms of Parkinson's. We went on with the exam, after which he said, "It looks like Parkinson's." He referred me to a neurologist, who gave me another exam. We made arrangements to have an MRI.

A Parkinson's diagnosis is not easy to make. Almost half of Parkinson's cases are misdiagnosed. The MRI ruled out a brain tumor. Based on my symptom presentation, my neurologist, Dr. Gross, ruled out essential tremor. My tremor happened when *not* doing tasks—it's called an "at rest" tremor. I had tried to compensate for my hand tremors on Sunday mornings by clutching the sides of the pulpit to make them stop.

Dr. Gross stated, "You have Parkinson's." Because I was still in denial, which is the first response to a loss, the diagnosis came as a shock. "It's a progressive neurodegenerative disease," he told me. "You will most likely die *with* Parkinson's disease, but you probably won't die *from* it."

I had planned to work to eighty, at least. Someone once quipped, "If you want to make God laugh tell him about your plans."

I was sixty-eight. My first question was, "How long will I be able to work?"

He turned the question back to me: "How long do you *want* to work?"

Given my new diagnosis, I responded, "About five years." As a Unitarian minister, I had no age limit for mandatory retirement—it was between me and the congregation I had served for twenty-four years.

He nodded in agreement, "You should be able to do that."

And I did.

Frank in the sanctuary at the Unitarian Church of Westport, Christmas Eve (2012).

To Have and To Hold From This Day Forward

My story can't be told without my wife, Lory. We had been married for twelve years when I was given the diagnosis. It was the second marriage for each of us, and we had achieved a balanced interdependence, emotionally as well as in tangible ways.

She did not typically attend church services. However, I always felt her supportive presence with me in the pulpit. Every Sunday morning right before I walked out the door, Lory would take me by the shoulders, look me directly in the eyes, and order, "You be great!" I always carried that energy and encouragement with me, which became increasingly important.

Frost's famous poem begins: "Two roads diverged in a yellow wood, / And sorry I could not travel both / And be one traveler, long I stood . . ."

The reality of my existence had taken a challenging turn. I was forced to take the Parkinson's road, a road with no choices or diversions. Parkinson's is a cruel taskmaster. It's like the mythological snowflakes—no two are exactly alike.

Parkinson's is a progressive disease, and it lets you feel its progress. It's one thing to have a tremor; you want to demand that your hand stop shaking, and it won't. It's another thing to be stuck, unable to move: ". . . long I stood." Would this be my path—immobilized and wheelchair-bound? I felt the loss of my autonomy and mourned.

A couple of years after my diagnosis, I heard about a Parkinson's support group in Westport led by Paul Green. Paul was in his mid-eighties when we met, and he had come to a deep acceptance of the reality of his existence, which had to include a space for Parkinson's for the last twenty years of his life. His motto was from Winston Churchill: "Nevah surrendah." He knew the difference between giving *in* and giving *up*. He never gave up.

I came to realize that I had plenty of choices to make. Choice begins with a conscious decision to embrace a deep acceptance of what *is,* as opposed to what you *wish* it were.

The experience of living with the disease is the teacher. As was Paul, and others I met who were dealing with life-altering illnesses. I also recognized that Parkinson's enhanced my ministry. The main ingredient of ministry is empathy. Although I always considered myself as highly empathic, I felt my new relationship to actualizing it.

Being one of eight children shaped my independence. From beginning my work life at age six to traveling across the country alone in a camper for six months on my sabbatical, my need for independence was always my M.O. Now, I found myself needing help.

At first, I felt robbed. But, like Robin Hood, I was rich in independence and poor in dependence. I gradually came to appreciate a sense of liberation from my own defining characteristic.

I have been blessed by my partnership with Lory. She watches the progress of the disease and responds carefully. She asks, "Do you need my help?"

Early on, I needed help buttoning my left shirt sleeve, since my tremor was in my right hand. After several years, my left hand joined the Parkinson's parade. I learned to button my cuffs before putting the shirt on. One must adapt.

Everything slows down, and sometimes it comes to an abrupt halt. That's one of Lory's challenges—patience. It's easier for me to have patience; it's forced on me.

I worry about becoming a burden.

Those six simple words sit silently like a tiger in the tall grass, waiting to pounce. Lory hasn't given me reason to feel like a burden. No one has. I wrestle with it.

Recently, I had lunch with a man who was ninety-nine years old. His one hundredth birthday was looming large. At one point, he said in a matter-of-fact tone, "I've had enough."

We sat in silence until I took the risk of breaking it with some lines from Walt Whitman's poem "When Lilacs Last in the Dooryard Bloom'd":

Come, lovely and soothing Death,
Undulate round the world, serenely arriving, arriving,
In the day, in the night, to all, to each,
Sooner or later, delicate Death.

Prais'd be the fathomless universe,
For life and joy, and for objects and knowledge curious;
And for love, sweet love—But praise! praise! praise!
For the sure-enwinding arms of cool-enfolding Death.

Dark Mother, always gliding near, with soft feet,
Have none chanted for thee a chant of fullest welcome?

Then I chant it for thee—I glorify thee above all;
I bring thee a song that when thou must indeed come, come
   unfalteringly.

Approach, strong Deliveress!
When it is so—when thou hast taken them, I joyously sing the
   dead.

Whitman's poem expresses his grief at the loss of Lincoln. Life is a series of losses for all of us. The so-called stages of grief begin with denial and move toward acceptance, which is a word used only with great caution, lest it sound like *approval.*

A Russian proverb says, "Why should we be happy when there are so many beautiful things to be sad about?"

Illness reminds us that we are mortal. A chronic illness puts a stopwatch on our screen. We hear the sound of the clock ticking, like the sound of the heart beating. Someday, it will stop.

The naturalist John Burroughs wrote a moving affirmation he called *Accepting the Universe.* In it, he said, "The laws of life and death are as they should be. The laws of matter and force are as they should be; and if death ends my consciousness, still is death good. I have had life on those terms, and somewhere, somehow, the course of nature is justified."

Sometimes, the raft we're floating on gets stuck in the mud, and we need a push.

LORY

When you love someone, you do not love them all the time, in exactly the same way, from moment to moment. It is an impossibility. . . .

Security in a relationship lies neither in looking back to what was in nostalgia, nor forward to what it might be in dread or anticipation, but living in the present relationship and accepting it as it is now.

–Anne Morrow Lindbergh, *Gift from the Sea*

"I'm going to marry this guy."

I had pulled up to the light at the corner of North Kings Highway and Main Street when the strongest sensation and "premonition" came over me. Psychic ability is certainly not something I profess to carry. But there have been a few extremely overpowering "truths" that I've experienced, which proved to be accurate.

It was October 1993. At the time, Frank and I had only been dating for a couple of weeks. Both of us had been separated for several months from our respective spouses, and we were eager to connect with someone else experiencing the same trajectory. We had known each other peripherally the year before each of us found ourselves single again.

When I moved to Westport in 1989 with my then-husband Bruce, we—both Jewish but not particularly religious—lived on a street with several families belonging to the Unitarian Church in Westport. We hadn't joined a synagogue and weren't feeling compelled to do so. Our UU neighbors would repeat enthusiastically how inclusive and special their spiritual home was. They emphasized how many members were

Jewish but felt comfortable with the interfaith and non-dogmatic tenets of the services. They raved about the minister.

We decided to attend a service. Moved by the beauty of the sanctuary nestled amidst the woods, as well as the dynamic and penetrating words of the minister, Frank Hall, we started attending more regularly.

After attending the church for a few months, I became pregnant. Shortly after the birth of my daughter, Carlyn, I decided to stop attending. Although I appreciated the focus of the church covenant on love and service, I could not escape the fact that it was a "church." I found myself seeking a reconnection with my Jewish heritage and culture, especially for the sake of my daughter.

Fast forward to 1993, and I was navigating a challenging separation and divorce process. I had a two-year-old to single-parent, a new but temporary living situation, and a job requiring me to commute into New York City. My friends were very supportive but could not relate. One of my friends, who had also been one of my former neighbors, informed me that the Unitarian minister was also separated from his wife.

I had some brief contact with Frank during the time I attended his church. There were a couple of times when we had an engaging conversation. Although I was impressed by his talent, his intelligence, and his innate ability to inspire and connect with his congregation, I wasn't sure if we would be able to relate to one another as individuals sharing a common experience. But the few times we had conversed in the past were evidence enough for me to imagine he could be a friend. So, I wrote him a note.

Frank responded immediately, which became the genesis of our relationship. Although we had an immediate emotional connection, it took a bit longer for us to establish ourselves as a couple. Premonitions aside, we each had our reservations.

He's a minister of a church!

I had stopped attending earlier because I couldn't reconcile my feelings about being a Jewish person who went to church. How could I be involved with a minister? Plus, he was (and still is) fourteen years older than me.

A grandfather! I have a two-year-old!

I know Frank questioned whether or not he wanted to be involved with someone whose primary responsibility was to her toddler, who was younger than his own grandchildren. Where would this lead? Did he want to go through this life cycle again? How would his children feel— they were closer in age to me than I to him. And we were both going through our own divorces, each trying for different reasons. Was this the right timing for a relationship?

Clearly, the answer was yes. For us, it couldn't have been better.

Frank was fifty-three and I was thirty-nine. At this juncture of our lives, having been through our own adventures and chapters, we had a sense of what would both bind and heal us. Starting off our collective journey with the stressors we were confronting served to lay a strong foundation for our relationship. We were lucky. Those stressors could have been our undoing. But we just worked really well together.

In 1995, we bought a house. I had been renting a condo in Norwalk and wanted to move back to Westport so that Carlyn could be in the same school system as her preschool friends. Frank wanted to be within close enough proximity to his office without being "fishbowl" close.

We have been living in that same house now for the past twenty-four years. Our house was built in 1929, a Dutch colonial: solid at its core, with distinct character, but open to change and growth to meet the needs of its inhabitants.

In Sorrow and In Joy

My mother died in September 1996, three weeks before our scheduled wedding at our house. She had been suffering from lung cancer for the past year, and the disease had been a shocking turn of events. My mother was not supposed to die from lung cancer. She had been diagnosed with lupus during her pregnancy with me. She struggled her

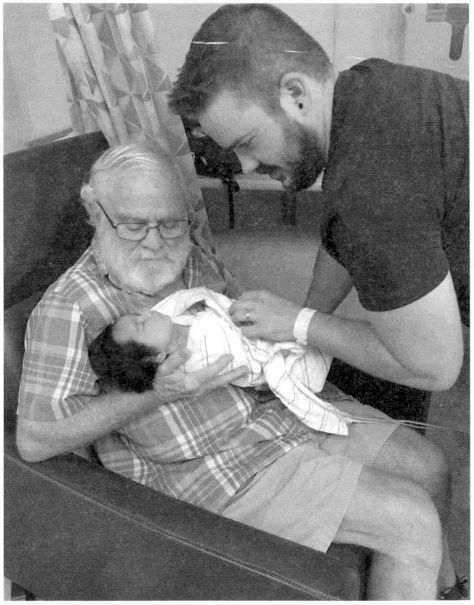

Frank holding his new great-granddaughter Sofia Jean Hildreth, with his grandson Alex Hildreth, Tufts Medical Center, Boston, MA (August 2019).

whole adult life with the impact that relentless flare-ups of this systemic autoimmune disease had on her body: attacking her lungs, her heart, her central nervous system. She suffered from chronic joint pain and fatigue. She was hospitalized countless times, many times near death, but she always managed to overcome her immediate crisis.

A product of her generation, she smoked cigarettes for years until, determined to quit cold turkey, she was finally able to conquer their ruthless control in 1981. Fifteen years without one puff, but her already compromised lungs relinquished to the power of cancer. She was sixty-five years old.

Wedding of Frank and Lory in their Westport home. The officiant is Herb Adams, a close friend and colleague of Frank's (October 12, 1996).

After their initial trepidation about hearing their daughter was involved with a minister who was significantly older, my parents quickly fell in love with Frank. My father, brother, and I will forever treasure the precious image of Frank tenderly reciting poetry to my dying mother—as he has done for so many of his dying congregants.

We planned our wedding fairly quickly, in hopes of my mother being able to attend. When it became clear she was moving closer to death, she had told me not to change the date. Knowing that we would be marrying was enough for her.

We were married in our house on October 12, 1996, surrounded by our immediate family and a couple of our closest friends. Joy and grief intertwined.

The excerpt by Anna Morrow Lindbergh which opens my story was read at our wedding. "Security in a relationship lies neither in looking back to what was in nostalgia, nor forward to what it might be in dread or anticipation, but living in the present relationship and accepting it as it is now."

It is challenging for me to remain present. I have always been a worrier, having one foot in "dread or anticipation." Frank has always been more naturally present, not dwelling behind or forward. But circumstance intervenes, and we have found ourselves in roles that demand to be defined by "as it is now."

More than a decade after we married, in 2007, I first began noticing Frank's second and third fingers on his right hand would shake while we sat on the couch watching television. The first few times, I ignored it. When the shaking persisted, I spoke up, thinking perhaps optimistically or naively if I brought this to his attention he could make it stop. Frank was aware, and he tried to stop the shaking, to *will* it to stop. With his purpose and focus, the shaking would cease momentarily before starting again. I knew what it was—not a premonition this time, but a "knowing." I didn't say it out loud.

I encouraged Frank to see his doctor, but he waited a few months, well into 2008, until he was concerned enough and convinced that something was wrong. His doctor strongly suspected Frank had Parkinson's disease and made a referral for a neurologist. The neurologist confirmed what I already knew. The tremors, now slightly more prominent in his right hand and also his right foot, the increasing difficulty he was having with handwriting, not swinging his right arm in natural synchronicity with his left foot while walking, even the vivid dreams he had been experiencing for years, were all confirmations.

Fortunately, Frank was considered to be in very early stages, and his symptom presentation had not worsened rapidly over the past several months. Parkinson's progression seems unique to the individual, so in the best case scenario, Frank would have many years of normal to relatively normal functioning.

It was at this juncture that I found my sustenance, my coping mechanism, which I fully embraced. I surprisingly was able to integrate and process this diagnosis by staying present with it. Not living out my usual M.O. of worry about what was our probable future—at least, not consciously. Just dealing with each step as it unfolded.

There was actually a feeling of comfort, having the diagnosis confirmed. We knew what it was and what it wasn't. And I experienced a strong wave of familiarity. I knew what it was like to live with a person with a serious, chronic disease. My mother had been terribly ill, sometimes deathly ill, from the day I was born. I knew what it was like to be a caregiver.

Was this random? Was this my "fate?" What was the universe telling me?

In the summer of 2009, I began a decade-long tenure with a hospice provider. I am a social worker, and I am fortunate to have had a varied and rich career. I was eager to embark on a new professional chapter, and this opportunity seemed like the right fit. Although I consider myself to be naturally self-scrutinizing and insightful, I can honestly say that until I started typing these words, it did not occur to me that in accepting this position, I was on some level trying to work out my underlying feelings of fear and dread about Frank's disease. I was aware of my own fears of death and how my work would help me process that, but I was completely out of touch about my subliminal need to process my feelings of helplessness about Frank.

I was, however, very aware that I would be confronted by the impact of the disease in its terminal stages on patients and their loved ones.

Some patients had been diagnosed many years before, and some more recently. Some patients suffered from Parkinson's-related dementia, which has been a huge fear of both Frank and me.

Witnessing the debilitation forced me to compartmentalize. I needed to be an effective support for the people I was serving, but I did not want to share what I was seeing and feeling with my husband. The person who had always been my source of support and my "ear" became someone I wanted to shield from the profound realities I was bearing witness to.

Frank worked for five years after his diagnosis. Although deeply rewarding, those five years were challenging at times, due to periodic work stressors that would exacerbate his symptoms, particularly his tremor. Always a vital and vibrant presence, he maintained his core spiritedness. However, his tremor deeply embarrassed him, as if it was emasculating. It was a physical display of how vulnerable he felt. I would always try to help him rally before a service, despite his tremor, as if my words could will him to forget or ignore its glaring presence.

In the summer of 2013, Frank retired. He left on his terms, all the while continuing to function at his best in the complex tasks of ministry. He never wanted to feel like he was compromising his congregation, or not have the ability to give them his all. He served his Westport church for twenty-nine years and his previous congregation for twelve years. A great run, a wonderful legacy.

Til Death Us Do Part

Retirement has created different challenges. Frank has worked since he was a young boy. He did not want to be a professional patient.

We had previously decided that upon his retirement, Frank and I would get a dog. Once this actually occurred, we engaged in a more realistic discussion about bringing a dog into our lives. Ultimately, we were convinced that having one was right for us. Not long after, our exuberant and precious Parker joined our family.

No, Parker is not named for Parkinson's, but for a Unitarian clergy hero of Frank's, Theodore Parker. (Although, on some unconscious level, perhaps . . . ?) In addition to being a bottomless bucket of joy, Parker has helped to give Frank a daily exercise regimen. Although not formally trained, he is the perfect therapy dog.

Frank, Parker (dog), and Lory in their Westport home (November 2019).

Like a cat working his way through his proverbial nine lives, my husband has endured a few other medical crises on top of Parkinson's. He had a hip replacement, which he very quickly recovered from. Indeed, his physical therapist fired himself, since Frank proved to be the model rehab patient.

The first, most serious incident was a stroke. The only presenting symptom was a balancing problem, and all of a sudden walking like a toddler or someone inebriated.

The MRI showed that he had suffered two previous "silent" strokes, a shocking discovery. When the neurologist came into his hospital room to discuss the MRI results, she thought she had the wrong room. She was so surprised to find the patient not completely debilitated. "You've had a stroke in a major part of your brain!" she exclaimed. When she spoke those words, I burst into tears and sobbed for a long time. I had been repressing so much fear and anxiety about Frank's mortality through the past several years, my defenses were shredded in that moment.

Once again, Frank made an impressively fast recovery. A couple of years later, he would be hospitalized once again, this time for a heart problem. He had been experiencing classic signs of an impending heart attack, but all his tests came back as normal. Fortunately, his cardiologist was convinced enough to take a look and found a ninety percent blockage in one of his major arteries. A certain heart attack was prevented with the insertion of two stents. He bounced back easily from this averted crisis as well.

Rather than acute, like the stroke and cardiac issues, the progression of his Parkinson's has been more insidious. At this juncture, Frank is still what I would consider independent, although he does need my assistance at times. Getting up from a chair, cutting up food, putting on clothes, or fastening a seat belt, for example, can present challenges. He fatigues easily and is overcome with feelings of weakness episodically. I would not hesitate to leave him alone for a few days, but not for longer. I still work, but have chosen a new position that enables me to have more flexibility with my schedule.

With these slow but steady changes in Frank's ability, I have maintained my focus to remain present and adjust to needs as they arise. I am well aware of the scenarios that are to come. We both are. And we will be prepared to manage his care. But it is crucial for me, emotionally, to take things one new reality at a time.

Throughout Frank's disease, I have found myself glaringly aware of my flaws. I have always considered myself a good partner to Frank, very loving and supportive and direct, not shy about challenging or confronting when appropriate. But the emerging manifestations of Parkinson's have tested me. I can never really know what it's like for Frank. I can feel compassion for him, but he is the one physically living it.

I'm aware that I have my own agenda of how to face chronic illness in exemplary style. In my mind's eye, my mother served as the poster child and model of courage and fortitude in the face of disease. So I need to remind myself at times to allow Frank to be human and not the mythological creation of strength in the face of adversity.

The biggest obstacle for me has been patience. I joke that it is not physically possible for me to relax. I need to be busy, always working, engaging in some activity, or making a plan. I can be still as long as it involves giving someone my undivided attention, and having a probing conversation of depth is probably my favorite thing to do. Parkinson's literally forces Frank to move at a slower pace. It can take him fifteen minutes to put on Parker's harness for a walk, and sometimes he can't do it at all. I try to balance his need for autonomy with my need to move more quickly. Sometimes, I manage to finesse this dynamic successfully, and sometimes not.

My biggest concern is not about Frank's increasing physical debility but about his emotional well-being. This disease has the potential to alter the foundation of our partnership. We have both recognized and embraced one another's independence. At the same time, we have not been afraid to allow ourselves to be dependent on one another—again, finding that balance. But that balance is in danger of shifting as Frank is slowly becoming more physically dependent on me. What will that do to Frank emotionally? Will he accept it, fight it, or will he become despondent and grief-stricken? What will it do to our relationship? I try to reassure myself that we have built a strong core and have always worked through our hurdles, ". . . living in the present relationship and accepting it as it is now."

If I am completely honest, I acknowledge that I miss our "old life," our more active life. We still have a lot of fun together, and we share the same slant on the world. But it is important for me to voice my losses as much as it is important for Frank to voice his. Not to look backward "in nostalgia" but to enable myself to accept what is now. And, if I am completely honest, what we have now is still everything I ever hoped for in a relationship.

We are one couple, and this is our love story.

FRANK HALL & LORY NURENBERG

Estelle Thompson (Margolis) graduates from middle school,
Public School No. 78 (June 1938).

Good Grief
• Estelle Thompson Margolis •

by Jonah Newman

THE LAST DAY I SPENT with my grandmother before she died was a sunny one in February 2019. Buba, my parents, and I were driving to the movie theater to see *Green Book*, which would win the Oscar for Best Picture just a few weeks later. As we turned onto Post Road from Myrtle Avenue, my mom got a call from her sister, Libby, the eldest of Buba's five children.

"Sarah's pregnant!" she exclaimed over speakerphone.

Libby's daughter was going to have a baby! Cries of congratulations bubbled around the car. When the noise died down, ninety-two-year-old Buba had her say at last: "F**king *finally!*"

Living to see her first great-grandchild was just about the only thing Buba—as I've always called Estelle Thompson Margolis—did not accomplish. Born to a poor Jewish immigrant family in the Bronx in May of 1926, she was an activist before she was ten years old, when she participated in a demonstration against the Japanese invasion of Manchuria outside Alexander's Department Store. She went on to be arrested three times for protesting the war in Vietnam and America's lax gun laws, and held vigil on the Ruth Steinkraus Cohen Bridge over the Saugatuck River every Saturday for some fifteen years. She would stand, despite her advancing age and bad knees, presenting signs that read "Bring Them Home" and "Truth Matters."

She taught union organizing at an integrated school in the South in 1947, where she and the students were under constant threat from the

Ku Klux Klan. Despite lacking an undergraduate degree, she was one of the first women ever to graduate from Yale Architecture School. She raised five kids with her husband, Manny, in their home on Myrtle Avenue in Westport, working as a full-time architect all the while and somehow also finding time to produce more than two dozen paintings, nearly twenty sculptures and collages, and hundreds of drawings. She sang with Pete Seeger, befriended Paul Robeson, Jackie Robinson, and Eva Marie Saint, and even once rode a motorcycle with Marlon Brando. By any metric, she was a remarkable woman, and became well-known around Westport for her kindness, generosity, tireless activism, and dedication to the community.

How does a woman like that reckon with old age, let alone mortality? How does someone like Buba—who left her parents' home as a teenager, took fierce pride in her self-sufficiency, and always lived life on her own terms—handle the physical limitations of aging?

In characteristic Buba fashion, she grabbed the bull by the horns. In 1997—more than two decades before her death—she created her *Good Grief* book. This was a binder full of documents, instructions, and resources to be employed "in case of." Buba's will and medical directives were there, of course, but so were detailed funeral and burial instructions, complete healthcare and prescription information, important phone numbers, proof of home and auto insurance, a financial appraisal of all the artwork she owned, and a handful of articles about dignified deaths, caring for elder parents, and alternative retirement communities.

Each of Buba's children was given a copy when it was first put together, and it was updated constantly thereafter, with new and revised documents added periodically until 2016. Buba also included a note to her kids at the very end: "If you have any questions, let me know." After her passing, a memorable moment of levity occurred when Buba's daughter Sarah (aunt of the pregnant Sarah from the beginning of this chapter) came across this note while browsing *Good Grief* for Buba's burial wishes. "We'll definitely let her know!" Sarah laughed. (It's that dark sense of humor that has allowed the Jewish people to survive centuries of persecution.)

To make the understatement of the century: Buba was not an apathetic person. She was known to have the table completely set for

Estelle Thompson marries Manny Margolis. She holds Manny's daughter, Libby, whom she would raise and love as her own (March 1, 1959).

her annual Passover Seders many hours in advance. (Granted, coordinating, hosting, and feeding her extended family was a titanic affair. But I think we all would have found a seat on the porch even without the name cards she set out for us.) Buba did things *her* way. She made a plan and then executed it. She set a goal and achieved it. So it was over the course of her life, from big accomplishments, like graduating from Yale, to small ones, like knowing the best way to fold a Band-Aid over a cut finger. Death was, to her, just another thing to prepare for. *Good Grief* was the natural and inevitable product of her conscious, intentional way of living.

But Buba's way was also the way of love. The primacy of love—the fact that really, it's the only thing in life that matters—was the single most important lesson I learned from her. Her huge heart allowed her to find warmth and joy throughout her life.

I believe that her attitude helped prolong her life. She had an infinite amount of love to give—to her children and grandchildren, to her friends and their friends, and even to people she'd never met. It was partially her love for children that spurred her to so vociferously agitate against war. The reality of twenty-something soldiers—"young kids!" she always called them—dying in foreign lands tore at her heart, along with the misery endured by others trapped in war zones. Her favorite necklace, which was buried with her, read: "War is not healthy for children and other living things."

Good Grief, then, was more than just a plan, more than just a collection of facts and numbers and legal documents. It was a gesture of love. It was her attempt to ensure that her death would be as hassle-free for her children as possible. Thanks to *Good Grief,* they knew the identity of her medical and legal representatives, where and how to bury her, how her estate would be divided, what taxes were due, and much more.

Dealing with the death of a parent is never easy—psychologically *or* logistically—but *Good Grief* certainly made the process easier for Buba's kids.

Although she was clearly prepared for death, she was frankly less prepared for aging. Throughout her life, she was used to complete self-sufficiency. Even after her kids were grown, Buba stayed busy. A typical day might include running errands around town (the Westport Library was almost always on the itinerary), cooking for herself and anyone else who happened to be in the house, writing her memoir, or driving to New Haven to visit the Yale Gallery or the architecture school. Even in her eighties and nineties, she would often say that age was just a number. "I don't feel it," she constantly asserted.

Her body begged to differ. Despite multiple surgeries, her hips and knees were in near-constant pain by the time she died in 2019. Several years earlier, she'd moved her bedroom from the second to the first floor of her house to avoid climbing the stairs.

I wonder if she was cognizant of the last time she visited the second floor, where all her children's bedrooms were located, or the third floor, where she kept her drafting table and art studio. Regardless of whether she had this closure, her loss of mastery over her home and her inability to visit all the spaces dear to her hit hard psychologically. So did having to use a walker, hosting a weekday caretaker, and forfeiting her Subaru station wagon when it became clear that it was no longer safe for her to drive.

Although these limitations rankled her, they allowed her to continue living on Myrtle Avenue, which was her top priority. However, as she hated depending on anyone or anything else, she would eventually take a risk and pay the price. Many times she tried to cover ground without her walker, fell, and ended up in the hospital with ugly bruises or even cracked bones. She would then promise us all that she'd be more careful, acquiesce to hiring an evening or weekend caretaker, go home, fire her caretaker without telling anyone, and fall again.

It might sound like a frustrating and miserable cycle, but Buba was prepared to pay any price to stay in her house and maintain some degree of independence. In fact, dying in her own home was exactly how she wanted to go. Her daughter Sarah once tried to convince her to convert

Estelle in her architecture studio on the top floor of her Westport home
(1980s).

her bathtub into a walk-in shower, so she could avoid stepping over the wall of the tub.

"You could slip and hit your head and die!" Sarah exclaimed.

"That'd be perfect," Buba replied without hesitation.

Although she failed to achieve her dream of hitting her head on the bathtub, she still went out in high style. After having a stroke some three months shy of her ninety-third birthday, she passed away peacefully at Norwalk Hospital on March 1, 2019. The date was her sixtieth wedding anniversary with Manny, who had died eight years before. I like to believe that their souls embraced on that day, reunited at last on the anniversary of their earthly union.

Manny and Estelle embrace at their 70th birthday party (spring 1996).

Aside from the date, the location of Buba's death also held significance. Her children were all born at Norwalk Hospital, along with my brothers and me. If she couldn't die on Myrtle Avenue, that hospital—the place where she became a mother, and where life began for so many of her loved ones—was a fine second choice.

After she died, we were confronted with a fact that usually goes ignored until it's directly relevant: it is extraordinarily expensive to die in the United States. We paid the funeral home thousands of dollars to take care of her body, to arrange the casket, to dig the grave at Willowbrook Cemetery, to lower her down on thick vinyl cables, and to fill in the hole again afterwards. The burial was dignified and the funeral director kind, but I couldn't help thinking about how they had us hostage.

Just like paying for healthcare, one essentially has no choice. Death does not discriminate, but the quality of a family's experience with this universal human event depends in large part on its financial means. Buba knew this, and included an article in *Good Grief* about the high cost of death. I'm sure she considered it another injustice worth picketing against.

Of course, the most memorable and profound aspects of the aftermath were without a price tag. At Buba's grave, her daughters, granddaughters, son-in-law, and grandson performed "Way Over Yonder" by Carole King, perhaps her favorite musician. The night before, we'd all convened impromptu on Myrtle Avenue and acted almost as if Buba had not died. We didn't let the reason for our gathering stop us from having a large, boisterous dinner party fueled by red wine and filled with laughter and music. After dinner, we gathered around the world's most comfortable couch in Buba's dining room, strumming guitars and singing songs by the Beatles, James Taylor, and Fleetwood Mac.

We didn't plan that little concert on the night before Buba's burial, but we all felt intuitively that it was the right thing to do. It was just like the dozens of family reunions, birthday parties, and Seders that Buba had hosted for fifty-plus years in that very house.

A month later, at the memorial party that my aunts and uncle organized, music filled Buba's house one last time. As the afternoon wore on, organized speeches and performances devolved into spontaneous conversation and song.

None of us had asked Buba before she died whether this was what she wanted at her memorial. We hadn't needed to. She lived so exuberantly that when the time came to memorialize her, there was no question about how. Her spirit sat with us that afternoon, smiling at her loved ones as we reveled in all that she embodied: music, joy, and love. It was a celebration of her life, not a lament of her death.

Estelle, age 92, with three of her grandchildren—from left to right: Henry, Matilda, and Jonah—less than a month before she died (February 2019).

Despite butting heads with her children over the balance between safety and independence as Buba aged, she always made her wishes clear, and her children respected them. At no point did they force her into a retirement home or impose life support systems on her, which would have extended her life but not, she knew, its quality. She was an independent, opinionated, passionate woman who lucidly communicated her plans and preferences. This made it easy for her loved ones to meet her on her own terms. When thinking about dying with intention and grace, it's hard to imagine a better example than Buba.

A graphic biography ESTELLE THOMPSON MARGOLIS by Jonah Newman

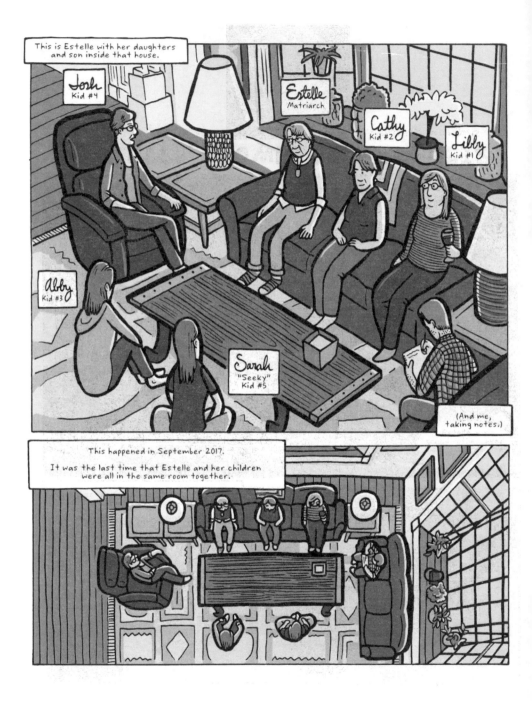

For my whole life, I knew Estelle as Buba.

She was an amazing woman.

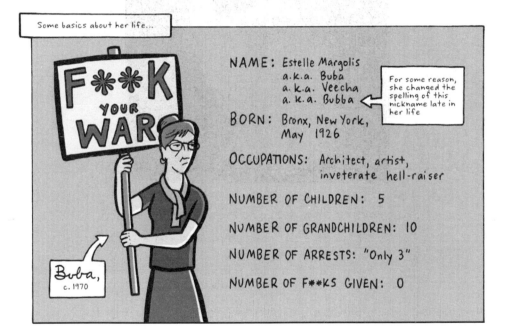

Some basics about her life...

NAME: Estelle Margolis
a.k.a. Buba
a.k.a. Veecha
a.k.a. Bubba

For some reason, she changed the spelling of this nickname late in her life

BORN: Bronx, New York, May 1926

OCCUPATIONS: Architect, artist, inveterate hell-raiser

NUMBER OF CHILDREN: 5

NUMBER OF GRANDCHILDREN: 10

NUMBER OF ARRESTS: "Only 3"

NUMBER OF F**KS GIVEN: 0

Buba, c. 1970

Accomplished, opinionated, and exuberant,
Estelle always lived life on her own terms.

She died as she lived:
with intentionality and grace.

Gerald Gross in his living room, library books at his feet (2014).

A Wonderful Life
•Gerald Gross•

by Sarah Gross

My Mother's Death

I WAS INTRODUCED TO DEATH and dying quite young. When I was eight, I almost died falling off a horse and rupturing my spleen. Then, at fifteen, I came down with spinal meningitis during one of the biggest snowstorms on record in Westport. I was delirious for forty-eight hours as the diagnosis became clear.

These two near-death experiences planted in me, unknown then, a kind of comfortable familiarity and curiosity about dying. It was not until I was thirty-two, when I was drawn to attend a symposium in New York City sponsored by the Omega Institute, did I start to understand the significance of my near-death experiences on my life and the lives of my loved ones.

At the time, my father, Gerald Gross, was sixty-three and a vice president in charge of the arts at Boston University. My mother Flora was sixty-two, a former president of the American Institute of Graphic Arts, and she began presenting signs of dysfunction. Her walking pace began to stagger. Then her writing became rigid and her thoughts harder to express. She was diagnosed with Parkinson's three years later.

The Omega symposium stuck a cord in me in relation to my own personal experience, and the experience of my whole family supporting a loved one through Parkinson's disease. It introduced me to American Zen Buddhist philosophy through the teachings of Roshi Joan Halifax and her wisdom of end-of-life process. Baba Ram Dass shared his *Be Here Now* revelations, Robert Thurman his interpretation of *The Tibetan Book of the Dead*, and Dr. Simcha Paull Raphael revealed Jewish beliefs of an afterlife. Presented with this expanded understanding, I felt met in a way I had not experienced before—where my personal experiences of death and dying at such a young age were finally given context.

My mother's evolving Parkinson's coincided with my father retiring from Boston University. My parents moved back to their beloved Greens Farms Road home in Westport, where my father began to take on the increasing demands required in the evolution of my mother's terminal illness. When he read about the experience of slowly losing someone to debilitating disease a little piece at a time, it gave him a much-needed orientation in how to relate to and understand the ongoing, helpless sense of loss we were experiencing as my mother slowly lost her abilities.

In Westport, I was able to be hands-on supportive. My mother was an accomplished cook; however, my father knew next to nothing in the kitchen. I began getting phone calls asking how to make pancakes or chop a red pepper. My bookish father even became proud of mastering the perfect bowl of oatmeal with honey, ginger, and warm milk.

As my mother's Parkinson's progressed, it became evident that my father needed more help and support. Navigating the stairs and magnitude of our home in Westport, plus the increasing needs of my mother, were no longer sustainable. At that time, there were no assisted living facilities in and around Westport.

My brother Adam, on the other hand, had a thriving architecture business in Baltimore and two small daughters. He had access to numerous assisted living facilities and loved the idea of Grandpa and Grandma being so close for him, his family, and friends. So my father— with an amazing burst of dedicated determination—began to feverishly pack up the home we all held so dear, eventually staging the most heartbreaking tag sale. The fabulous things of my mother's graphics collectibles, the art of our extended family and antiques, were sold off as she remained oblivious to the tragedy being witnessed by us both. The house—my mother's expression of self—was sold, and they moved to a somewhat sterile, two-bedroom assisted living facility in Baltimore.

Thus began the challenge of my long-distance relationship with my family, and my intention to be of service in the midst of running my own thriving catering, events, and prepared food business in Westport, Cabbages & Kings.

We talked often. My father would tell me about navigating doctors' appointments, lugging wheelchairs in and out of cars, changing diapers, changing bedding, making meals, all in caring for my mother. It took significant persuasion for him to finally admit that this was too much for a single person, and eventually caretakers began a daily routine of caring for my mother.

One night, when my mother was at my brother's home being watched over by their housekeeper, she fell and had a stroke. She was hospitalized with blood on the brain. I immediately drove to Baltimore. It was here that I was first introduced to my Great Aunt Roz. She was in her nineties, a comedian, and of all things, a self-professed psychic. She proved to be a wonderful support to both my father and me. While my mother was still in a coma, Roz said that she could still hear us and to tell her that we were right there with her. We all would be okay if she wanted to let go and find the light.

Once again, I felt met in this unknown realm by an aunt who knew the way, helping to create in me even more capacity to understand the process of death and dying. The stroke severely compromised my mother's ability to communicate, yet she was still there underneath. Inspired by the vision of finding the light, I created a painting entitled "Stairway to Heaven," which hung as a visual prayer over my mother and father's bed.

My mother had a rich end of life due to the care and involvement of my father and the close proximity of my brother, sister-in-law, their two daughters, and all their friends. She died quietly at home while my brother and I were en route to her. On the plane, I chanted a Buddhist prayer to aid in her passage, taught to me in that Omega symposium.

When we arrived, arrangements had been made to remove my mother's body. I insisted we sit with her for some time—my brother, father, and I. My father talked about how her drifting off to death had been slow and quiet, like she was floating down a river in a canoe. We also talked about next steps: going to the crematorium to make arrangements and the memorial service.

Opening the front door the next morning, a huge, dark grasshopper sat on the railing. It seemed larger than life as it climbed up my arm, greeting me before it jumped away.

At the reception after my mother's memorial, we arrived to the buffet covered in little green grasshoppers. It was magical and surreal. Then arriving to my own home weeks later, what first caught my eye was the Asian print of a garden hanging above my fireplace that had belonged to my mother. It was as if I was seeing it for the first time. It was full of grasshoppers!

Grasshoppers often have to do with faith in leaping forward without knowing where, like when we die. When they appear in my life, often in my garden, I am reminded of my mother and the joy she took and shared from her own luscious garden.

My Father's Life

My father had a wonderful life.

Gerald Jeremiah Gross was brought up by his loving grandmother in Union City, New Jersey. His parents, immigrants from Austria-Hungary, separated when my father was quite young, to make other lives for themselves. His father had a hat store in Queens and remarried, taking on the family of his new wife. His mother moved far away to Los Angeles and also remarried.

We would see my grandfather every so often on a Sunday. He would bring hats from his store for dress-up, and fabulous onion bread from

Queens for our Sunday brunch. We rarely saw my grandmother.

The city of Manhattan became a great part of my father's life from the time he was sixteen. He found a rich community to engage with, who loved books and the opera as much as he did. They would go to readings and concerts and gather back at one person's house afterwards for cheesecake.

In line at the opera was where my father met the artist who would later be my godfather, Lewis Dean. Then, when my father was nineteen, he was invited to a party honoring the Marquis de Sade. He became smitten with a stunning, free-spirited, eighteen-year-old Hunter College student named Flora Finn. They married soon after, and Lewis helped my mother sew her wedding dress.

When the war called, my father immediately enlisted. The camaraderie he experienced as a navigator flying B-24s as part of a bombing squad over England and Germany was life-changing. The experience was pivotal in contributing to his passion for history.

While my father was at war, my mother developed an interest in typography. Returning home, he was encouraged by my mother to take a class in publishing at City College of New York. He began as an editor at Reynal & Hitchcock. From there, he went to Pantheon Books and Harcourt, Brace & Company, finally landing at Macmillan Publishers Ltd in charge of the trade division.

As our family grew, my brother arriving three years after me, our extended family grew too, becoming one of authors, editors, and artists. Robert Penn Warren rocked me in my crib for hours. Ralph Ellison held me in his arms when I was an infant. Amos Sewell, a Saturday Evening Post illustrator, and his salt-of-the-earth wife, Ruth, were like our grandparents. We summered with them in Maine. Their house was our home away from home, and our Christmas dinner was always shared.

Albert Erskine, James A. Michener's editor, and his elegant wife Marisa and daughter Silvia, now a local landscape architect, were often at our Thanksgivings. Our house was filled with woodcuts gifted to us by Antonio Fasconi. He and his wife Leona Pierce, also an established woodcut artist, were a part of our clan, too. Graphics of esteemed designer Paul Rand graced the walls of our home. He and his wife Marion were guiding lights in my life. This extended "family" all lived in and around Westport.

With my father in publishing and my mother involved with graphics, books of all kinds, even books of criticism, always surrounded us when we were growing up. My brother and I never had to go to the library because our home *was* one.

At sixteen, my class from my Quaker boarding school spent the night at our home as part of a field trip to New York City. They were in awe, spending hours rummaging through the shelves and shelves of books, discovering art, history, and the like. (They were equally in awe of our overflowing refrigerator and eclectic garden, my mother being an avid home cook and gardener.) It was in those moments that I began to step back, in order to take in the abundance of our lives that I had taken for granted until then.

I had never been that close to my father. He worked and traveled a lot while I was growing up. Our classic photo is him at the family dining table behind his newspaper. Later, as my mother progressed with Parkinson's and he retired to Baltimore, we became very close, getting to know each other while caring for my mother.

One of the things that always amazed me about my father was his ability to vibrantly recreate himself: from publishing in New York, to being a vice president for arts, publications, and media at Boston University, to founding the Huntington Theatre there.

In Baltimore, he recreated himself yet again. He began giving talks on publishing and often courted writers he discovered with an idea for a book, while at times authors came to him. With his close connection with Boston lawyer Ike Williams, my father established himself as a literary agent under the auspices of Jill and Ike's full-service literary agency, Kneerim & Williams, which my father encouraged Ike to found in 1990.

Clockwise from top left: Elaine Lustig Cohen (graphic artist), Arthur Allen Cohen (Judaic scholar), Gerry Gross, and Flora Finn Gross (1959). Elaine and Arthur were two of the extended, creative "family" welcomed by the Grosses into their home.

My father also made a connection with Dan Rodricks, who was an NPR reporter, and they became good friends. He befriended Carla Hayden, now the Librarian of Congress, who then headed the Enoch Pratt Library in Baltimore. Our family piano was given to the Enoch Pratt Library in his honor.

My father passed on his knowledge and love of life not only to his family, but to our friends, too. Both my friends and my brother's friends would inevitably leave a conversation with my father having something to think about. We consistently received clippings from him on topics we were interested in, or helpful advice through an email or phone call. He was always eager to share inspirational insights that he thought would be of value to friends and colleagues alike.

So when he discovered that his Jamaican housekeeper in Baltimore, Cindi, had a twelve-year-old son, Housani, who needed help, my father offered to tutor him. Housani, very shy and reserved, would come once a week to work with my father. This became a very precious friendship for them both as Housani grew into a very proud young man. In turn, my father helped Housani get a full scholarship both to Loyola Blakesfield High School, and then to Albright College in Pennsylvania, where he graduated with a business degree.

In addition to helping others, my father loved music. When he read about the young Russian piano prodigy Ivan Moshchuk attending the Peabody Institute in Baltimore, he arranged for Ivan to give a concert at his assisted living facility. From there, my father became one of Ivan's biggest fans, and Ivan became a part of our family.

Book of Days

Amazon packages of books and CDs were constantly greeting him at the door. The glass coffee table once broke from the weight of books piled up on it. Without Tower Records in Boston to get lost in for hours, the immediacy of an Amazon delivery helped feed this passion. Every nook and cranny of his home was filled. At one point, when I commented on the endless stream and that he really needed to stop, my father said books were his friends, music got him high.

Couldn't argue with that.

Clockwise from top left: Perry Gross, Mathias Meguma (Ugandan exchange student), Kyle Gross, Adam Gross, Fredye Gross, and Gerald Gross (2012).

Several years after moving to Baltimore, he began to have more difficulty moving around, bought a scooter, and took on a walker. After a close call, when he totaled his car returning home from the library, he stopped driving. Frustrated with not having this constant access to books, he adjusted by arranging a library truck to arrive weekly at his facility for everyone's use. He loved compiling a weekly list of new finds as the piles of library books sat at his feet by his living room chair.

I began to spend more time in Baltimore, asking questions, taping the stories of his life. Each time I found him with his head in a book, I asked him, "Dad, what are you reading?"

One time, it came as no surprise to me when the answer to that question was Atul Gawande's *Being Mortal: Medicine and What Matters in the End*. He read passages to me from it, saying, "Ain't that the truth" and "Yes, that is how I feel." We were able to talk quite frankly about the many aspects of death and dying, especially getting used to *being* without *knowing*. Which you can imagine was a particular challenge to a man who craved knowing as much as he possibly could.

When not visiting him in Baltimore, we talked almost daily over the phone. Hearing music blasting in the background when I called—opera, classical, blues, ragtime, you never knew—was always a good sign.

He befriended Henry, a local record shop owner. They shared a vast love of music and stereo equipment. Even with the steep stairs up to the shop, my father braved his way there. And in his inimitable spirit of wanting the best for each person he connected with, my father suggested Henry start hosting concerts in his downtown space to help make ends meet. Henry, in turn, was often a guest at my brother's Sunday suppers, as were other of my father's friends.

My father's ninetieth birthday was a wonderful celebration, with friends far and wide attending. That birthday was a turning point for him. He began a more directed focus towards the end of his life and, much to my surprise, claiming his legacy became of utmost importance to him. My vision of my father was always as a "back of the scenes" kind of guy, a cheerleader, bridge builder, and connector. But with my mother dying so early and his progressively limiting ailments, my father was certainly aware that his time would come.

My father's legacy was twofold. One, it was key that he was formally recognized as a founding member of the Huntington Theatre Company in Boston. Since it was founded in 1982, the Huntington has received over a hundred awards for its productions, including the coveted Tony Award for Outstanding Regional Theatre. There is a plaque in his name there, and the directors still miss him and his input, which he continued to offer throughout his life.

Two, it became very important for him to record his experience in publishing Albert Speer's book *Inside The Third Reich*, which he accomplished in an NPR interview with Dan Rodricks. It was also imperative for my father from the start, if he were to be involved in publishing Speer's book, that a significant portion of the proceeds from the book go to survivors of the Holocaust. Speer agreed.

What I found astonishing about my father's experience with Albert Speer, who was Hitler's architect, was how having a record of this history was by far more important than the man himself and the atrocities he participated in during WWII. Their relationship rose above that as they talked together about the collective trauma of the war and even socialized. Going to a concert together, Speer warned my father that they would get "looks."

My mother was not as comfortable, and this was not easy for her. This connection between my father and Speer, however, significantly expanded my understanding of the overriding importance of recording history, and the nobleness that my father embodied: a Jewish descendant speaking with a key ally of Hitler.

Each time I would visit my father in Baltimore, I would gather more video. My father's memory was astounding. I loved hearing stories about hanging out with E.E. Cummings in his younger days. Or when George Orwell was not happy with the cover of the paperback version of *1984*, and my father had to go into work on a Sunday to rectify the situation. And then his encounters with Marlene Dietrich, wooing her to write her autobiography—she never wrote it and had to return the deposit.

He spoke about his friendship with the historian Barbara Tuchman, and contemplating taking tap lessons when he was in between jobs. My father loved flamenco, and he loved blues. His collection of all kinds of music was astounding. He held a deep gratitude for his life. Sharing his curiosity and passion was a mission. For him, there was always going to be a tomorrow.

At ninety-three, he began to have close calls falling and found blood in his urine. He was eventually diagnosed with small cell bladder cancer. This is a fast-moving disease. He had two operations to try to remove it, yet it spread fairly quickly.

Gerald Gross in front of a B-24, the same plane he flew in WWII.
Picture taken at an exhibition at Dulles Airport in Virginia (2011).

Gerald and Sarah Gross on vacation in Martha's Vineyard,
where they took family trips from when the children were
young, and also afterwards as adults (2011).

It became important for my father to meet the attending rabbi John
Franken at the local synagogue to talk about his final memorial. He
brought CDs, and conversation quickly morphed from the task at hand
into a lengthy discussion of music. After that meeting, the rabbi would
spontaneously call to talk to my father or stop by out of the blue to see
how he was doing. Even with my father not being particularly
religious—except on Yom Kippur, when he became privately pensive—
this connection gave him significant comfort.

As cancer began to prevail and my father's pain grew more
intolerable, pain meds were given. Hospice was called in to monitor,
and the rabbi began more visits to his home, sitting by my father's
bedside singing Hebraic songs. Most amazing was how my father
calmed with the rabbi's singing. Unfamiliar became familiar, as lineages
of lifetimes were being addressed, remembered, and included with the
vibration of these ancient words being sung.

With the increasing pain medication, my father's cognition of the world became unstable. He started having nightmares. He hated them. The moment he was not able to be present and in connection, he wanted out. He started saying he wanted to float away in the canoe, our code language for death. He was done.

As he knew his ending was nearing sooner rather than later, he began to hold court in his home. Visits were scheduled so he could say his last goodbyes. He took on the elegant energy of a Buddha. Very aware that these meetings would most likely be his last, he became very clear and deliberate with his sharing.

When celebrating his ninety-fourth birthday at my brother's home, he spent special time addressing my nieces, his grandchildren Kyle and Perry. You could tell that this was an effort, yet it was important for him to give his last blessing to them. Holding Kyle's hand, he said, "Where you start out may be a long way from where you finish, so you are a lucky, lucky girl and have so many opportunities. You do not know where you will end up, so that makes every day incredibly exciting."

It was very touching to witness. He died three days later.

At my father's memorial, my brother and I, Dan Rodricks from NPR, Ike Williams from Kneerim & Williams Literary Agency, and Housani, whom my father had mentored, all spoke. Ivan drove all the way from Detroit to play the piano, and we had bagpipes play "Amazing Grace" as we exited the service, since my father loved bagpipes. Housani wore a bow tie—given to him by my father, who loved bow ties—and recited William Ernest Henley's poem "Invictus" that he had learned with my father.

> Out of the night that covers me,
>   Black as the pit from pole to pole,
> I thank whatever gods may be
>   For my unconquerable soul.

In the fell clutch of circumstance
   I have not winced nor cried aloud.
Under the bludgeonings of chance
   My head is bloody, but unbowed.

Beyond this place of wrath and tears
   Looms but the Horror of the shade,
And yet the menace of the years
   Finds and shall find me unafraid.

It matters not how strait the gate,
   How charged with punishments the scroll,
I am the master of my fate,
   I am the captain of my soul.

Both Dan and Ike talked about how my father was a mentor to them, the father they wished they'd had. Though hearing this makes sense, it was surprisingly moving to witness the deep, significant effect my father had on these two grown men's lives. My brother talked about my father's history, and I spoke about the intimacies of his life.

When thinking about the prospect of my father dying years before, I thought I was going to not be able to cope and would need friends by my side to hold me up. Such a significant loss was unimaginable. Instead, the miracle for me has been just the opposite.

After the memorial service, my brother and I took on the monumental task of going through my father's belongings. As my brother sorted through his papers, on occasion reading aloud what he found, I looked through thousands of books, CDs, and records. My father's life began unfolding and expanding even more. Handwritten quotes were left in drawers, as if for us to find and reflect on. Clippings were found in books, at times adding different dimensions to them. The over 6,000 CDs and records, expressing my father's passion with music, were a lesson in themselves when I sorted through them. Blasting the

Red Hot Chili Peppers or contemporary bagpipe music, by far, gave me and still gives me the greatest joy: celebrating my father.

My mother used her home as an expression to define who she was, through the eclectic nature of her choices and in how she cooked and took care of us. This was her salvation. My home and my gardens have become my salvation in ways that are my own.

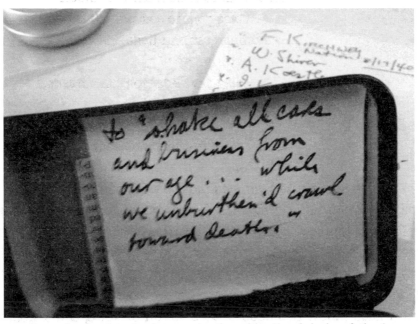

One of many handwritten notes found by Sarah in her father's home after his death (October 2015).

I am not a musical aficionado by any means, but studying vibration in relation to healing is a current passion of mine and clearly feels like my father's love of music is coming through me in that process. When I witness myself sharing the wisdom of the moment with others, I feel my father. When I notice my capacity for bridge-building, seeing the essence of someone when they might not, I feel my father. When I pursue my interest in collective trauma, I feel my father.

Both he and my mother live on in me. My father, too, lives on in the many lives he chose quite deliberately to touch.

After the memorial, I asked Ike Williams for a copy of what he'd spoken at my father's service. He told me, "I had no notes. I spoke ad hoc, as the Romans when honoring their heroes. I miss him still."

Michael Maso, managing director of the Huntington Theatre Company, wrote words about my father that continue to resonate with me, as they would to anyone who knew him.

"He was a great friend and mentor, and he changed my life's path profoundly for the better. We are all in his debt."

Anne Beers' last week, toasting with a mix of (mostly) water and wine (April 2019).

The Veteran Optimist
•Anne Beers•

by Jarret Liotta

FOR ANNE COLE BEERS, IT was never about clinging to life, but about embracing it—throwing her arms around a vibrant and multifaceted world with clear, open eyes. She lived absent of expectations or judgment, but instead with sincere gratitude and a spiritual philosophy rooted in ongoing hope.

After delighting in, and sometimes enduring, all the motley episodes populating her personal timeline, after tasting each experience and relishing the wide range of events and feeling a full spectrum of emotions throughout the rollercoaster process of living, she went forward into her final chapter with characteristic ownership and conscious engagement. She experienced her end-of-life on similar terms.

For decades, it had been Anne's unyielding intention to die at home surrounded by her family. Despite a long and healthy life led into her nineties, she'd regularly told her children and grandchildren for decades that this was what she wanted. Though on random occasions, her request was modified to include, for a finale, merely being pushed out to sea on a small boat and left to disappear over the horizon—southeast of her beloved Marblehead, Massachusetts, where she would ultimately rest—she still remained steadfast in her main plan. She wanted to be surrounded by loved ones, to toast them with laughter and a final goodbye, and to cross over with quiet acceptance from the comfort of her own bed in her own home in Westport.

In each case, it was always clear she knew what she wanted. Unlike many people, she appeared to recognize an ironic simplicity in crossing over. As she'd lived her life with a matter-of-fact presence, resolute in her beliefs and behaviors, quietly firm in her humane convictions, so too did she leave the world with contentment, a clear sense of purpose, and utter practicality.

Anne Cole came to life with a positive outlook abetted by a strong sense of self, which was a far less common trait among women in 1924 than today.

Picture the crisp, breezy coastline of Massachusetts Bay, and the nearby, inland settlement of historic Winchester, Massachusetts. It was a fitting home for a branch of a New England clan that had come over on the Mayflower some three hundred years before. The family was well off, and Anne, the youngest of three, enjoyed the trappings of a well-cushioned home throughout her early years—servants, comforts, and an easy sense of security.

Perhaps more importantly, Anne's parents, Sam and Georgianna, were a relatively broad-minded couple. They encouraged not only her strong sense of identity, but Anne's desire for education, as well as the requisite work ethic that she wholeheartedly embraced. There was no need for a gossamer dream to draw her forward in life, as the path was forged even before her journey began.

Her parents and environment instilled in her a strong sense of fairness and justice, coupled with an attitude of patriotism deeply rooted in her ancestry. She was the product of a rare kind of household that allowed room for her exceptional confidence to flourish.

Unfortunately, fortunes didn't last for Samuel Cole, since the Great Depression wiped out his business enterprises to a great extent. The impact was understandable and, while there was still the remainder of a fair life the family could fall back on, Anne's ease and comfort were largely thwarted.

But her general resiliency was not.

Anne at Marblehead, MA in her early twenties.

"How lucky can I be?!" Years later, Anne wrote this in a note— again and again, over and over—and pinned it on the refrigerator or shared it with her friends and family. As life's verities splashed over the sides of her vessel, as the decades passed and she experienced her share of heartbreak, disappointments, and disillusionments, she regularly and repeatedly made a conscious choice to focus on the full half of the glass.

Up until the end, notes on her refrigerator remained a handy way to help her sort out perspective on life's ups and downs as they came her way, putting into columns daily reminders to keep steering her ship toward brighter horizons.

My septic went kaflooey.	It didn't back up into house!
I had a car accident today.	Could have been killed —wasn't!
Bank is foreclosing on new house.	I didn't want to retire anyway!
Real estate market is lousy.	Gave me more time to goof off!
Had a rotten 1989.	Only 17 days 'til 1990!

There was always something to appreciate and for which to be grateful. Throughout her many years, Anne consistently demonstrated this example to those around her. She was never one to try and impress her opinions on family or friends with words, but instead kept her beliefs in practice. A devout Congregationalist since birth, and later a dedicated attendee at her Greens Farms Church in Westport, Anne lived her spiritual beliefs in a private way. As a consequence, her guiding influence on those who were closest to her, as well as so many others she met in passing, was always subtle and quiet.

The tenets of tradition—American tradition in particular—were also pivotal to Anne's development. "We came over on the Mayflower, and we are patriots. My family has been patriotic forever, and . . . my Marblehead house is all red, white, and blue," she said once, referencing the home her grandfather built on Cloutmans Lane in 1891. She purchased the house from her mother, and it was where her own extended family would visit over the summers.

When World War II was in full force, Anne chose to leave college without fanfare, enlist in the Navy, and follow in the footsteps of so many family members—including her brother Donald, who was in the Army, and her sister Patricia, who was in the Marine Corps. Anne was assigned to the U.S. Navy Hospital Corps and stationed in Portsmouth, Virginia. She served as a pharmacist's mate from 1944 to 1946 and gave her hand in direct care to hundreds of wounded service people.

"You had to be twenty years old to enlist as a girl," she once remembered more than seventy years later. "I was stationed at Portsmouth, Virginia at the general hospital. I was a psychology major in college, and they wanted me to deal with sailors coming back from Iwo Jima who were mixed up in their heads."

Anne's darkest memories centered on overnight bedside duties in which she tried to help others as they crossed over. "I had to sit at night duty in the hospital with people who were dying, and it was hard," she said. "I felt so bad, and there wasn't much I could do except comfort them. That was my worst memory."

But she also experienced incredible camaraderie. "We were all in our early twenties and we had fun," she said. "We all laughed a lot. We all fit. We loved it. We felt we were doing something important, but we had fun along the way [and] we knew we were going to win the war."

"We all had a sense of humor," Anne noted. "You have to have a sense of humor in this world."

Despite the verities of military life and the intensity of her work, she forged strong bonds with several people, ones she maintained over half a century. According to her beliefs, they are destined to continue even beyond this plane. "Most of them are no longer living and that pains me, but I'm gonna see them up there," she once said, pointing toward Heaven.

Representing the Navy at The World War II Memorial in Washington, DC on Memorial Day several years ago.

Following the financial challenges that had come upon the family in the wake of the Great Depression, Anne took a job in Boston at General Electric in her late teens in order to help pay for her college. She began her studies in Pennsylvania at Beaver College, later renamed Arcadia University. After her 1946 discharge from the Navy, the G.I. Bill gave her full tuition to complete her degree at Tufts University, where she majored in psychology and ultimately graduated magna cum laude. There, too, she met her husband-to-be, a fellow Navy veteran and

Massachusetts man named Rowland Austin "Junie" Beers, whom she married in 1947.

Times were different then. From a distance, Anne's life appeared to develop the way of many middle-class ladies of her era during the 1950s, though she was a noteworthy exception for both her psychology degree and her veteran status. The couple settled southwest of Boston in a town called Wrentham, where Anne gave birth to three children—Daniel, Natalie, and Janet. For the most part, she focused her attention on their activities, even helping start the first kindergarten class in town for her eldest.

In 1964, Anne loaded the station wagon and drove her kids down to East Texas to join her husband, who had taken an HR job with Texas Instruments. Richardson, just northeast of downtown Dallas, was a much different place than Massachusetts—from its segregated stores and restaurants, to its fear-driven attitudes regarding people of color and those who abetted their integration.

During their first days down there, the family arrived at a Texas Laundromat. Apparently, the signs sent them into two different rooms depending on whether they wanted to wash their whites or their colored clothes—or so they thought. Actually, it was just a segregated Laundromat, and became a memory burned in the family's consciousness. Something they had hardly imagined or ever encountered before.

True to form, Anne didn't set out to make a stand regarding her own beliefs, strong as they were. At the same time, steadfast in her core values—and perhaps as immovable as the granite foundation of her Yankee heritage—she didn't yield to the mores of that Southern lifestyle but went intentionally about her business regardless.

As she began establishing herself in real estate in Texas—a career she would adore for close to fifty years—Anne discovered some opportunities through her husband's work in human resources, in particular helping some of his new employees settle down in the city. Early on, this would include the first African-American man—a bright, young engineer with unique skills—to be recruited by Anne's husband, who needed to find a home to go with his new job.

Anne and "Junie" Beers (a.k.a. Rowland Austin Beers).

All of Dallas housing at that time was segregated, and trying to change those historic traditions was tantamount to troublemaking. And yet Anne, with no zealous emotion, simply understood that the best home for this black man was in a white neighborhood. And so she moved forward, breaking ground in the arena of fair housing.

For months, she received harassment, including anonymous phone calls where she would be called virulent names. Yet Anne didn't back down and, moreover, simply wasn't that fazed. After all the arrangements were finally made, the man simply bought the house. The bullies evaporated—perhaps cleansed through Anne's matter-of-course determination that it was simply going to happen whatever people tried to do—and then, anti-climatically, she heard no more about it. She continued on in her work and became a very successful Realtor throughout the region.

By the early 1970s when they arrived in Westport for good, Anne had established her expertise as a top-notch Realtor. She would often state that she was soundly aided by her background in psychology, which she saw as a distinctly valuable skill for sales. "What they said they wanted in a house, and what they really needed and wanted, were two different things," she noted. She took the time to talk to her clients, to actually listen to them and discover what was really at the heart of their search for a new home. As a consequence, she developed strong relationships with many of them—became "best friends with everyone," according to her son—and enjoyed multiple repeat customers over the course of decades, as well as making a lot of very good friends around Westport and beyond.

And Westport was a town that Anne took to immediately, in part as a refreshing change from the periodic struggles she saw in the South, but also because of its likeness to her Massachusetts home. It was a Northeast community with hearty cold seasons and breezy summer times by the shore. As she had in Texas, Anne loved to be involved with the children's activities—Brownies and swim teams amongst them—as well as the community at large, taking part in a variety of causes and institutions, in particular those that related to women's interests and ideas on equal rights. She was part of the Westport Woman's Club, the Westport Sunrise Rotary, the Y's Women, the Green's Farms Association, and the League of Women Voters, among other local groups.

When she wasn't lending a hand to this range of causes, working, or caring for her kids, Anne took part in regular poker games with several other women Realtors in Westport, some of whom became her closest friends. She prided a quick mathematical mind, which lent itself nicely to her love of bridge as well. It was a game she even enjoyed on the computer up until the end of her life.

Between the weekly games, get-togethers, traveling, and myriad community activities, Anne led an active social life for decades, both before and after her divorce at the end of the 1970s.

Despite her many progressive values and outlooks, ending a thirty-two-year marriage had never been on Anne's radar, in part because of her core beliefs in the permanency of family. New, unwanted independence and all the complicated trappings of a messy breakup took the wind out of her sails for a long time. And while she harbored some understandably strong resentments against her ex, true to her core character, Anne still kept walking forward, taking on new responsibilities in raising her children, and eventually her grandchildren. Despite the daily strains and struggles encountered, she always sought to focus on what was going well at any given time in her life, rather than the problems she had to face.

As she drew closer to the end of her life, Anne came to peace with the very few people she had long, lingering resentments toward, most notably her ex-husband. Whether it was a direct result of her faith or an adjunct to just growing older and leaving the material world behind, in the end—despite their contentious divorce and many subsequent years of hostility—she demonstrated a sincere forgiveness toward him. During her last dying days, Anne even claimed to see Junie standing before her—re-experiencing the depth of their historic connection—and

From left: Daniel Beers (Anne's son), Steve Cavazuti (Janet's partner), Rick Davies (Nat's husband), Nat Davies (Anne's daughter), Janet Beers (Anne's daughter), and Anne Beers.

spoke happily to her children of ultimately meeting their father again beyond this life.

For Anne, the end came quickly, but that's a relative term. At age eighty-nine, the same year she finally retired from William Raveis Real Estate in Westport, she was misdiagnosed with colon cancer. She and family members found the diagnosis "a little sketchy," according to her son. Thankfully, on the advice of a friend, they sought a second opinion that revealed it was actually uterine cancer. Anne was sent in for surgery immediately at Yale New Haven Hospital.

While the work of her surgeon gave her good odds post-surgery, Anne was still faced with pursuing treatment afterward. Following the surgery, she paid a visit to the infusion ward, where she saw the people receiving their chemotherapy treatments. She was due to be next.

"I'm not doing this," she said bluntly. "I'm going home."

Doctors tried to talk her out of it. The oncologist stated that without the chemical follow-up, she would die within six months to a year.

But Anne was adamant. She never went to see another doctor again after that.

In consequence, she continued her life unabated for five years in total, slowing down her pace as she entered her nineties, but experiencing no significant issues related to that diagnosis until about a month before her death.

⚬⚬⚬

Anyone with firsthand experience at the bedside of an individual passing on will attest it's not a particularly smooth and easy process to be a part of. It's not like TV or the movies, insofar as it's sometimes slow and drawn out. It's exhausting, it's emotional, and it's imperfect.

The physical stages of dying experienced by the individual also correlate to a complicated and somewhat unpredictable series of emotional stages felt by friends and family in close proximity. While it may be a wonderful concept in theory—the chance for any person to meet their end in the personal comfort of their home—it's simply not the best option for everyone.

The Westport-based Beers family was fortunate, however, for an ample team of extended family and close friends was jointly willing to endure the challenges of seeing this inimitable matriarch into the next life. It was a frank request Anne had made starting decades before, and as she saw her time was imminent, she again made it clear that this was the ultimate gift they could give her.

She was ready to go. "I've had enough," she said as the days wound down. "I've done everything."

Her loved ones noted that she often spoke of seeing her sister and couldn't wait for the chance to be with her again, as well as others from her past. Most importantly, as she expressed both directly and indirectly, she knew in her heart that everyone she would leave behind was going to be okay and was going to be taken care of. Anne sailed into the proverbial sunset of her dying process with a clear sense of relief that she had done all she needed to do, and that those she was leaving behind were well equipped for her parting.

Anne's close friend Sharon Carpenter played a key role. A former nurse, she'd been through this kind of experience many times before. She lovingly augmented Anne's care, qualified to administer medications. Sharon also understood various and inevitable phases of demise, so family members were afforded firsthand knowledge of what to expect even if, at times, it might prove uncomfortable, disheartening, or simply sad.

Witnessing the body's failure and the broad and varied stages it encompasses are, especially for someone who has never seen them, disconcerting at best. While Anne's family members never wavered from their conviction that they had made the right choice in helping her exit the way she had always seen fit, it still took its toll on each individual.

The last week, Anne experienced tremendous pain and decreased mobility. A wheelchair was rented to get her outside the day before she died, but even after getting down the one step into her first-floor bedroom was an exhausting production for family members. Gratefully, none of them had to face those responsibilities on their own or in isolation, and so they bore the worst parts.

"It was a lot more difficult than I thought it would be," her son said. "It was all-consuming, more than any of us thought it would be."

Fortunately, it wasn't all stress and sadness. Her children, grandchildren, and great grandchildren were afforded the chance to give and gain comfort with her, to build direct closure on their relationships, and to simply laugh together and toast life. Anne raised many a glass in her final days—watered-down chardonnay, with generally a lot more water than chardonnay—a spirited spirit who saluted life and all its faces during these various, final visits.

Amidst the goodbyes, Anne was never shy about broaching the subject of death itself. She spoke of it often, exhibiting no fear around the concept. On the contrary, her adamant belief in an afterlife brought comfort to her family, as did her overriding spirit of joy during those final days. Death shouldn't be dreaded, but a spiritual exercise worthy of a hands-on experience.

Spending time with Anne during that process, they came to truly feel that there is, in fact, something much more than this life we know. They were honored to be privy to an up-close look behind the curtain.

When Anne finally left on April 20, 2019 at age ninety-four, it was on her own terms, the culmination of her journey and the product of her personal power, replete with a legacy of positivity and satisfaction for a life well-lived. Her family was able to keep its promise to her that they wouldn't isolate her or move her somewhere else, and she appeared to make the most of this unique experience.

"She never stopped saying how grateful she was, and that was the best gift of all," her daughter remembered.

The family continues to process her loss and leaving. Her remains were brought to the family plot adjacent to her Marblehead home—her favorite place—at her request. While some tears remain, there's also a general sense of wonderment at the process that they witnessed. Further, owing to a wide-ranging series of coincidences experienced, some of the family members are quite sure that Anne is still nearby in spirit, actively connected to them each and every day.

Clockwise from left: Anne Beers, Kim Barna (Janet's daughter), Janet Beers, Lindsay Miller (Nat's daughter), Abby Heirtzler (Janet's daughter), Nat Davis, Carrie Gallagher (Janet's daughter), and Katie Martin (Daniel's daughter).

Sharon noted that, among the many people she had known and seen pass away through her work and personal life, her friend Anne was visibly the most joyous among them—comfortable and confident, happily resigned to her fate with a palpable sense of completion. "She had it figured out," Sharon said.

And Anne's own words continue to resonate as the most fitting salute to her spirit and the intimate connection she shared with those around her.

"I've had the best life!"

Mathew Kleiner (2002).

Everything is Definition
•Mathew Kleiner•

by Robin Weinberg
with Jenny Kleiner

MATT KLEINER AND JENNY BUTLER met as first year law students at NYU in 1993. Matt was tall, six feet two inches, blond, really good-looking, with that natural charisma that drew people to him. Jenny is beautiful and sweet, with a calm energy that belies the way she speaks a mile a minute. Jenny and Matt became best friends pretty quickly.

They were just friends until their third year of law school, when word started to spread that they had taken the leap and become "More Than Just Friends." The common reaction was, "What took you so long?"

After graduation in 1996, they got an apartment in New York City and their first jobs as attorneys: Jenny at a corporate law firm and Matt at the Manhattan District Attorney's Office. They were married in September of 1997. On New Year's Day 2003, Jenny gave birth by C-section to triplets Abby, Sam, and Megan after twelve weeks of couch rest.

A few months later, while the babies were still in the NICU, Matt died from complications from HIV and hepatitis, both of which he had lived with since he was eleven.

His diagnosis at such a young age impacted how he lived, the choices he made, and the causes he fought for. At his death at age thirty-one, he was a husband, a father, a friend, a prosecutor, a health advocate, a political activist, a change-maker, and a model for how to live fully and deliberately with the uncertainty of a serious illness.

This is Matt's story in Jenny's words, as told to me, their law school classmate, in several very long conversations over very large coffees.

Jenny

I remember the moment I first saw Matt. It was practically the first day of law school at NYU, and I was going out to a bar with some new friends. I walked in, he was sitting in a booth near the front door with a bunch of other first year law students.

I noticed him right away. I can still picture him sitting there. He was just so cute. And he was tall. And he was very . . . not loud . . . but a very commanding presence. He got your attention. At least, he got my attention.

My friends knew them, so we went over and all started hanging out.

Turned out, we were both in Dean John Sexton's constitutional law class. It's funny because every year on the first day of class, Dean Sexton would say, "Look to your left, look to your right; two of you are going to get married." And I was sitting next to Matt. So I guess it was meant to be.

At the time, he had a girlfriend, Jodi, who wasn't at school with us but was around a lot. They broke up a few years later.

Dating him wasn't something I ever thought about; we just spent a tremendous amount of time together as friends. And he was one of my best friends. Jodi was, too, and still is one of my dearest friends. Looking back, I thank God they stayed together as long as they did because I love her, and our friendship wouldn't have happened if they had broken up at the beginning of law school.

I don't remember Matt telling me he had HIV, and it wasn't ever the first thing he told people, but somehow everyone in our law school class knew.

Matt was born with hemophilia A, a genetic disorder that prevented his body from making a particular protein called Factor VIII. Without this, Matt's blood could not clot properly, meaning that the scraped knees, bumps, and bruises that are a normal part of any little boy's life had far more serious consequences for him. They could cause dangerous internal or external bleeding, chronic joint pain, even death. Any time Matt was injured, he had to have an infusion of Factor VIII. When he was very young, this meant frequent hospital visits, and maybe even an overnight stay.

Drug companies made Factor VIII from the blood plasma of volunteer donors. Back in the early 1980s, donors weren't screened, and donated blood wasn't tested or treated for viruses. The medicine was made by first dumping blood from hundreds of donors into huge vats. Mixing all this blood together meant that a single donor's contaminated blood could infect countless people.

This led to widespread infection among the hemophilia population of two viruses: HIV and Hepatitis C. When reports of the tainted blood supply started to surface, hemophiliacs, including Matt, were called in to their doctors for testing.

When his results came back, Matt and his family learned that he— along with ninety-five percent of hemophiliacs in his age group—tested positive for both Hepatitis C and HIV.

He was fourteen years old at the time.

Jenny

Matt told me that his doctor sat him down to tell him, "Here's what you have." And also told him, "Your goal is to live until you're thirty, and after that we will be able to keep you alive." Which is ironic, because it's probably true—short of the opportunistic infection that he got, it probably would have been true. He died when he was thirty-one.

When his family found out, they decided not to tell anyone. At that point in time, people thought it was like having the plague. He used to tell me a story about being in gym class sometime after he found out. And the teacher had an apple sitting on a table and someone took a bite of it. And when the teacher came back into the room and saw it, he was angry and said something like, "This isn't funny. I could get AIDS this way."

I can't imagine having that kind of huge secret. But I think it would have been worse if everyone knew.

When Matt was in college at Cornell, he kept a low profile at first. He would go to parties where the other kids would drink too much and wind up sleeping with some relative stranger. And he started thinking, *If you did that with me, you could get HIV*. It made him nervous, knowing what he knew about himself, and how it could happen to other people, too. And he wanted to help people, help them protect themselves.

When he was a college junior, Matt decided to go public. He started talking to everyone about HIV and the risks. Eventually, in conjunction with the Health Education Office at Cornell, he developed a safe sex education program.

He first delivered his presentation about safe sex to thousands of students, staff, faculty, and the local community at Cornell. Then he presented it to his law school classmates at NYU and other colleges and high schools in the area, including Staples High School in Westport, Connecticut.

He could pack a room and work a crowd. His presentations were wildly popular and incredibly hilarious. They were up front, in-your-face, practical talks about the importance of safe sex, how to do it, and how to make it fun. He came with pocketsful of props: condoms, dental dams, tubes of lube, sex toys, etc. His mission was not to scare or embarrass people, but to normalize safe sex and the conversation around it, regardless of whether someone was gay, straight, having casual sex, or in a relationship.

Sharon Dittman was the Associate Director of Cornell's Health Services. She wrote to Matt's family and friends when she found out he had died:

His matter-of-fact approach, comedian's timing, sex-educator's frankness, counselor's sensitivity, insider's knowledge of Cornell student life, and occasional well-placed impatience made him an extraordinary educator. He resisted the temptation to turn his programs into the "Matt Show," usually preferring to work with a partner in conducting workshops with Cornell students; and he had some great ones! He also refused to allow his audience the distance, comfort, or pity that might have come with casting him as "innocent victim" and often was intentionally ambiguous about his sexual orientation and his source of infection. A heterosexual man and hemophiliac who was infected as a child, he fought just as hard against homophobia and sexism as he did for personal, relational, and social change on a campus, in a world living with HIV.

Jenny

He started his presentations by saying, "You could walk into a bar and pick me up and you wouldn't think twice about it. I don't look dangerous. You wouldn't think that I have something that you could get that could be deadly." His idea was: *If I can save one person from getting infected, I am a success.* I'm sure he probably saved a lot more people than that.

A lot of people asked me why I would date him. They were worried about me getting involved with someone who might not live a long time and who could infect me, too. I understand the question, but—he was an expert in safe sex, right? In fact, somewhere in my closet, I still have one of Matt's books, *Safe Sex for Dummies*, which my kids think is hilarious.

When we started dating, I would worry about it once in a blue moon, but I think you figure that as long as you were safe, you would be okay. Or you should be, but that's also not a guarantee.

I would always say to people when they asked me why I went out with him, especially people who have been married twenty-plus years, "Would you change anything? Would you not have married your husband if you had known?"

It's hard to know, but I really believe that people would make the same decision I made. They just weren't put in that position. They maybe can't imagine making the same decision, but I think they would.

So, other than his sex ed talks, having HIV was not a focus for him. It was just a part of who he was. I don't think he thought of it as this thing that was hanging over his head. I don't have the impression that it occupied his mind all the time.

It did affect his career choice, though. He wanted to be a doctor. But he thought that medical school and residency would be too taxing on his body, too exhausting for him. And, of course, he wondered whether anyone would actually want to be seen by a doctor with HIV.

So he decided on law school, figuring he could still help people. Plus, he was just so brilliant—the work in law school came easy to him. Not for me! But he never had to worry about it being too hard on his body or his brain.

Maybe two weeks after we started dating, Matt started having some weird symptoms. It was kind of ironic—he was fine until right after we decided to get together. He suddenly couldn't walk well; his right foot was dropped. So we went to the doctor. It was one of those funny things where they said, "It could be leukemia. We're not sure." They found some lesions in his brain. And we thought, *Leukemia. That would be so awful.*

Graduation party in New Jersey (late 1990s).

It turned out to be PML, which wasn't leukemia, but also wasn't any good at all. PML is progressive multifocal leukoencephalopathy. It's an infection that attacks white matter in your brain. Actually, lots of people have it, but their immune systems fight it off, and so most people never have any problems. But Matt's immune system was weak. So he couldn't fight it off.

He went downhill pretty quickly. In a pretty short time, he couldn't really walk at all. And it was scary because we learned that you get this, and six months later you're dead.

Despite this, Matt finished his third year of law school in a wheelchair. He was chosen to be our class graduation speaker. Graduation was held in the smaller arena in Madison Square Garden. Five thousand people, including a few hundred of us in NYU violet caps and gowns, watched Matt as he wheeled himself onto the stage to give his speech.

Jenny

I remember him in his wheelchair at the podium. He was hilarious. And inspiring. The wheelchair itself was inspiring, because it was a message that, "If I can do this, then whatever it is you're worried about, and whatever it is you think you can't do, you can."

Matt knew he could be this inspiration for other people, and I think he liked that. He liked being helpful. He wanted to make a difference. You know, I'm pretty sure he would have liked to be President; I'm sure he would have gone into politics had he survived. I don't think I would have been a very good politician's wife, but he would have definitely wanted to do it. He loved to help people, to inspire people; he got a kick out of that.

His opening line was, "One of the most important things I learned in Dean Sexton's constitutional law class, other than the fact that venue is not jurisdiction," this is a law joke that I really tried to get him to take out—he didn't listen and, of course it got the biggest laugh, "is that everything is definition. A death sentence is only a death sentence if you define it that way."

I honestly think he believed this.

After we graduated, we moved in together to an apartment on the Upper West Side and started studying for the bar exam. Matt's friends started researching alternative therapies for PML. They found some studies that said that if you take Zovirax in super high doses, it can help with PML. Matt's attitude was, "What the hell? I'll give it a shot." At the same time, he started taking protease inhibitors, an HIV medication.

Walking over the Brooklyn Bridge (2000).

It was amazing. Somehow, he got better. He ended up walking with a crutch for the rest of his life, but he was better. By the time we finished our bar exams and started working, he was out of the wheelchair.

It was an against-the-odds recovery. PML is not something people survive, much less bounce back from. Matt almost fully recovered, except for the partial paralysis on his right side. He had to make some changes in his life and career path again. He switched from the trial division to the appellate division at the District Attorney's office, because he thought his body couldn't keep up with the rapid-fire existence of a trial attorney. He commuted to work in car services; the subways and buses were not accessible enough for him.

And yet, at the same time, he taught himself how to swing a bat with one hand so he could play on the DA's softball team.

Jenny

He wasn't a complainer. I only remember one time. It's funny it sticks in my head, because I don't think I ever heard him say it again. This was after he was out of the wheelchair, he said something about how it sucked that he couldn't do everything he wanted to do. That's it, just one time. I would always ask him, "How are you feeling? How are you doing?"

Finally, he said, "You have to stop asking. I'm fine."

I really don't think he ever thought that having HIV would impact how long he lived. Sometime after we were married, he said something about maybe only living until his sixties. It was startling, because he had never said anything like that before. Frankly, I never thought about it, either. Because he was such a strong personality and so full of life, it was hard to picture him not here.

In 1997, Matt and some organizations and lawyers representing hemophiliacs began uncovering some startling truths. Drug companies were able to, but weren't, screening blood donors to identify high risk donors, and they could have, but opted not to, ensure that any HIV and hepatitis viruses in the blood plasma supply were killed with a simple heat-treatment process. The latter, they argued, would have doubled the price of Factor VIII for hemophiliacs.

Hemophiliacs who wanted to sue the manufacturers of Factor VIII for these failures faced a huge legal obstacle: the statute of limitations was only three years. This means that Matt would have had to sue within three years of the blood test that confirmed he had HIV and hepatitis when he was fourteen years old.

Daniel (nephew) with Matt at Jenny's mother's home in Westport (2000).

In New York, a bill was pending that would open a window of time for hemophiliacs with statutorily expired claims to file lawsuits. There was also, at this same time, a class-action suit, which had negotiated a settlement payment of $100,000 for each hemophiliac, dead or alive, who had been infected.

Accepting the settlement payment meant waiving the right to sue. Rejecting the settlement could mean losing all options of compensation from the manufacturers if the New York State bill didn't pass.

Matt decided not to join that class and take that settlement. Instead, he got to work.

Jenny

We went up to Albany together—Matt, his dad, and me. There was a big group of other hemophiliacs there. We were milling around at this building as the legislators were coming by on their way to vote on the statute of limitations waiver. I think we had signs, but I don't remember what they said. Lobbyists for the drug companies were there, too.

Funnily enough, one of the lobbyists for the drug companies was a guy Matt had known as a kid, a family friend. He was trying to fight the passage of the waiver. And Matt was standing there. He had his crutch, and his right arm and his right leg didn't work. So, this guy came up and said, "Oh, my God. It's so good to see you! I remember when you would run around my yard as a little kid."

And Matt, classic Matt, his response was, "Oh, yeah? You remember that? When I had two arms and two legs that worked?"

Matt just shut him down. The guy slinked away. We couldn't believe that he—or anyone—could take the side of the pharmaceutical companies. Matt said to me, "What possible reason could he think that this bill isn't fair? They may think that we don't have a good case, but we should at least have the right to give it a shot."

The waiver passed. And Matt sued the pharmaceutical companies.

I can't go into details because he wound up settling. The money really helped. It took the financial burden away, at least initially.

Matt couldn't work at a law firm. He couldn't have worked at a job that paid lots of money and work those crazy hours. His medication and doctors were expensive. So I think the settlement gave him some peace of mind, in the sense that he felt he was contributing and taking care of his family even when he wasn't working any more.

But this whole thing was important to him to fight for because he wanted justice for the hemophilia community. Because this shouldn't have happened. I also think he wanted people to realize that telling the story about the failures of the drug companies could help people stay safe, could stop this sort of thing from ever happening again.

To that end, Matt also called up a friend from his Brooklyn neighborhood, documentary filmmaker Marilyn Ness. He pitched an idea to her: a documentary film about how 10,000 hemophiliacs were infected with HIV from tainted blood products.

The film, completed after Matt's death, is called *Bad Blood: A Cautionary Tale*. It explains how, at first, people wrongly believed that the decimation of the hemophilia population was a tragic and unavoidable accident. But it goes on to show how the drug companies failed to use, and government regulations failed to insist upon, the heat-treatment procedure. This could have saved the lives of thousands of people. Matt appears in the film as one of the faces of this tragedy.

Jenny

Marilyn was a family friend of Matt's from Brooklyn. He approached her because he wanted to get the information out, have people understand the story. Other than Ryan White, most people didn't know about hemophiliacs with HIV/AIDS. It is an incredibly small population, but it was a huge percentage of them who got infected.

Matt also wanted to tell the story of how this tiny community really banded together. They rose up and fought back against these drug companies. Matt was a very strong believer in doing the right thing. And it's obvious that the drug companies didn't do the right thing.

Matt knew that Marilyn could help tell that story. Marilyn worked on the film, on and off, for about ten years. It was released in 2010. It was quite a labor of love.

In 2001, Matt left his job at the DA's office to manage Dave Reiss's political campaign. Dave was one of his closest friends from law school, who decided to run for City Council in Brooklyn. What made Matt think he could run a political campaign is beyond me. He had absolutely no experience. But it was amazing. Honestly, Matt thought he could do anything.

He talked the talk of an experienced campaign manager. In an article in the May 11, 2001 *New York Law Journal*, Matt was quoted as saying, "Politics should be a combination of passion and vision and know-how." This same article referred to Matt as "the youngest and perhaps the most passionate of an earnest bunch." It also mentioned his tough decision to leave his job at the Manhattan District Attorney's Office. "I was doing something I really enjoyed. I was helping people on a case-by-case basis, but not enough people."

When asked what would happen if Matt's candidate lost, he said, "I want to parlay this experience into a career, as an administrative aide to someone. I'm not thinking of becoming a candidate myself, not with my health situation. There are too many days when I wake up and say, Oh I really don't want to go out to the train station and shake hands."

Jenny

Dave didn't win the primary, ultimately. But he got a significant amount of votes, and I remember thinking, *That's amazing to get all these people to vote for someone!* I mean, it was really incredible!

At the same time, Matt and Jenny had started working on what would become Matt's living legacy: his three children. They found a fertility clinic that used a sperm-washing technique to scrub away viruses and went through several rounds of IVF treatments before Jenny became pregnant with triplets. Her pregnancy was complicated, and the babies were born ten weeks early on New Year's Day 2003. Shortly after, Matt's health started declining rapidly. He went into the hospital while the triplets were still in the NICU.

Matt and Jenny with niece Amy at Jenny's mother's home in Westport (2000).

Jenny

Matt started to get disoriented because his liver function was so off. I remember he got up in the middle of the night, and he was talking but not making any sense. We went to the hospital and they said that they couldn't believe he was as coherent as he was, given that his liver was failing, basically.

It's funny because, if I remember correctly, a liver transplant could cure his hemophilia. But they couldn't give him a transplant because they'd have to suppress his immune system even more, and then the PML would kill him.

I was visiting the babies, and in the hour I was gone, the doctors told Matt and his father that there was nothing more they could do for him. The only good thing—a silver lining maybe?—about me not being there is that Matt got upset. I don't know if he would have gotten that upset if I was in the room. He always tried to protect me and, in fact, he never actually said anything to me about the conversation with the doctor.

I know he said to his dad, "Who is going to take care of my family? Who is going to take care of Jenny and the babies?"

I wanted him to come home—I thought he'd be more comfortable. But he wanted to stay in the hospital. I don't know if he felt safer there, with doctors and nurses around, or if he didn't want to die at home. It's all a blur.

But I was with him when he died. I find it very weird. I had a cot, so I slept there the whole time he was in the hospital. And the night he died, well, he died in the morning. But for some reason, I got into bed with him. I was sleeping next to him.

I remember, I woke up and his breathing had changed. So I have this impression, did he want me to wake up? Did he somehow wake me up? Maybe I just heard it or just happened to wake up?

I don't know. And then he stopped breathing.

Matt died on February 27, 2003. His funeral at Temple Israel of the City of New York was standing room only. Jenny's sister, Susan, and several of Matt's closest friends from college and law school, Rob Fromberg, David Rosenberg, and Dave Reiss, gave eulogies. Jenny also asked people to write memories down for the triplets, who are now seventeen years old and juniors at Staples High School.

Jenny

It's hard raising kids by yourself, and I feel like I've had my fair share of flops. But I feel one thing that I did a good job of was keeping Matt alive for them, especially because they never actually knew him. They know him through stories they've heard—that their dad got married, had kids, and had a career. He did all this stuff as if there was nothing holding him back. He had the attitude that he would be around for a long time.

Or maybe the idea of the worst thing that could happen had already happened. So why not just enjoy life to the fullest? It would've been lovely if he'd made it to eighty-five, but this all made him who he was.

I have a copy of Dave Reiss's eulogy. He said, "I have told many a person that Matt is the finest man I have ever known. I am devastated by our loss. But I feel blessed to have known him for ten years; I will cherish my memories of him, and I will continue to be inspired by his example of a life worth living."

When I think of Matt, I think about how he lived like he was never going to die.

He lived like there was always hope.

Allen Wasserman on guitar, in concert with friends at Rockwood Music Hall.

Relative Perspective
• Allen Wasserman •

by Craig D.B. Patton

RECEIVING THE NEWS THAT YOU have a serious health condition is life-altering and scary. Receiving a cancer diagnosis eighteen months later and being told you may have only three months to live is unfathomable and devastating. If the person who received such news then raged at the unfairness of the universe or plunged into a deep well of depression, it would have been understandable. Allen Wasserman did neither, a testament to the pragmatism that always defined his life.

A partner at Locke Lord, one of the nation's top law firms, Allen was initially diagnosed with heart disease and told he had eighty percent blockages in his blood vessels. Surgical procedures were ruled out. He went on medication and made changes to his diet to reduce his cholesterol. But none of that mattered anymore when, in 2016, he learned he had stage 4 gastrointestinal cancer and given three months to a year to live. Over three years later, having beaten the odds, he shared his story during a series of conversations at the Westport Library, Temple Israel in Westport, and his Weston home.

Remembering back to the initial days and weeks after his diagnosis, Allen recalled, "I never had the 'Why me?' moment. My grandfather, who was a Polish immigrant, used to sit me down on the couch that he made. And whenever I complained about anything, he would say, 'Allie boy, Allie boy. So, what can you do about it?' And if I told him there was something that I could do, he would say, 'Are you going to do it?'

If I said yes, he'd say, 'Good. Good luck.' If I said no, he said, 'Then what's the point of complaining?'

"And I always took that view, that it's just not a good use of emotional energy or time to dwell on things that you can't change. So, once I was diagnosed, I just accepted it. I didn't like it, and it was a shock, and it was traumatic, and of course all of the things you would expect. But I just said, 'Okay, this is it. Now I'm going to deal with it.' "

His first concern was for his wife, Lory, his daughter, Danielle, and his son, Matthew, both of whom were young adults. Allen was only in his late fifties and wanted to ensure their security. A few consultations with his lawyer and financial adviser convinced him that all would be well on that front.

An additional relief was that the leadership team of Locke Lord were extremely supportive. "I had a good relationship with the chairman of our firm. I called her and before I could really finish saying what I was going to say, she said, 'You know, I feel terrible for your family. If there's anything we can do, let us know.' And she said, 'Do not worry about your numbers. You're getting a one-year pass. Do what you can do. Focus on the things you need to focus on, and we'll deal with things down the road as it becomes necessary.' "

As he moved through a series of chemotherapy regimens to fight his cancer, it eventually became clear that the high time and energy demands of his law career were no longer a good fit. He decided to transition to disability.

The new challenge: what to do with all of his free time? He started by focusing on projects around the home that usually went ignored. The mystery contents of file boxes stacked in the basement or stashed in corners were identified and labeled. The decluttering of the house that Lory had been eager to tackle progressed. But Allen realized he needed to take a radically different approach to life.

"I had always thought that in my retirement—which I envisioned would have been ten years later—I would explore my creative side and work on my artwork. And I realized that I actually didn't want structure. I decided just to be cognizant of the things I knew I wanted to do, but not to a schedule where I was creating any stress for myself."

During his legal career, Allen had developed an interest in mixed media artwork, assembling works from seemingly incongruous pieces. Now, hc had the freedom to make regular trips to as many area stores as he wanted. He scoured shelves and raided clearance sales. He stockpiled chair legs and metal letters, holiday ornaments and household items, plates of glass and bits of pipe. With no timetable and with the chemotherapy treatments sometimes slowing him down both physically and mentally, the shopping trips were often prolonged. "A ridiculous amount of time was spent at Home Depot and Lowes, nurseries, consignment shops. Just looking at things and trying to figure out, okay, will that help with this project? Maybe this gives me an idea?"

Lory was bemused. "She would ask me, 'How many times do you need to go to Peter's Market?' " Allen recalled, "Or, 'Is that all you did today?' " But Allen's definition of what constituted a plan or defined progress had changed. "It literally got to the point where I would assign myself one or two tasks that I kncw I wanted to perform. If someone wanted to know my plans, I would say, 'I'm going to wake up in the morning, and if I wake up, I'm going to take it from there.' So, if it was a nice day, I would be out in the garden, working on projects in the garden. Maybe go get the car washed. Sometimes, I would just go out with no destination in mind. Just to drive around streets in the neighborhood that I had never thought to turn down because I never actually had a reason to, and I thought, 'Well, I might as well do it now.' And it was great, because I have no sense of direction and I get lost all the time, and here I couldn't get lost because I had no destination. So that was it. It was just a very non-structured period."

As a self-described loner, the time spent on his art suited him. But his family and friends continued to suggest events to add to his calendar. And Allen decided that finding a reason to say yes to their loving generosity was important. "There are too many life experiences we miss out on because we don't take advantage of the time we have and seize the moment."

One friend sent him to a racetrack where he drove an exotic sports car. Another sent him to Foxwoods Casino. Another, who was a pilot, took Lory and him on a trip to Block Island and Cape Cod, having a different meal on each. He guest-hosted a New York City radio show. He fronted a band made up of musician friends and played a sold-out show at Rockwood Music Hall in New York City. Despite having no 'bucket list' of his own, Allen was pleased to find himself filling one provided by others, saying, "I have done some amazingly fun and interesting things."

Allen and wife Lory enjoying a helicopter flight in Hawaii.

His friends were also the impetus for holding a F**k You Cancer dinner on the first anniversary of his diagnosis. "And I really didn't want to because that's not my thing, but we talked about it, and it did occur to me that it had been a pretty remarkable roller coaster of a year. I wanted to thank my friends and just celebrate life." He and Lory turned it into an annual summer event, when they held a festive but casual outdoor dinner party featuring a live band playing rock and blues.

A larger project was the chance to hold a show at Silvermine Art Guild featuring his work. It was an exciting opportunity, but one that came at a cost.

"It was the most stress I had related to my artistic endeavors because, suddenly, a deadline had been injected into the process. And I had to negotiate details with the gallery director and others." The sheer logistics of the event—how to transport, load in, and display his artwork, how to light his works in a gallery setting, how to quickly break down and remove everything—became daunting.

"And then one day I stopped myself, and I said, 'No, you're not going to take on anyone else's stress and anxiety about this. I can do this. I know what I need to do.' " He finished preparations for the show in a mad dash. "I pulled the college all-nighter. I set up the basement as a shop, the dining room as a studio. I had the garage going. I had everything going. And I was jumping from one project to another, and the place was a pigsty."

In the end, he exhibited thirty pieces, and almost a hundred people attended the show. They deluged him with praise and questions about his work.

"I was stunned," he said. "It just all came together. It was a great night. It was absolutely unbelievable."

But all the while, largely invisible to the many people in his life, Allen's battle with cancer continued. Chemotherapy treatments worked for a while and then failed. Severe bouts of pain followed, until the next, more severe treatment took effect. His medical options ran low. "And that's when I had the limbo moment where I thought to myself, 'This is a tough way to live.' The not knowing from one week to

Allen with his family at his gallery show (June 2019).

another. None of us know how long we have, but when you're diagnosed with cancer, you're suddenly focused on your mortality."

Allen at Temple Israel with his art piece, entitled "A Light Unto the Nations."

He looked at all the wonderful experiences he'd had since his diagnosis, all of the art he had created, all of the tennis he had played, and understood how blessed he was. "Only ten percent of the people with this cancer are alive five years later. I'm not kidding myself. I know that I've been fortunate. I also realize that it's not just that I've been around this long. My quality of life has been excellent."

He realized that just because he did not know how much time remained was no reason to change who he was or how he had always approached life. There was no way to control what was happening, so he would not waste time or energy worrying about what came next. "Live for today. Do the things you can do today and just focus on that, and if you start a project that you don't get to finish because you pass away, so be it. And if you end up living long enough that you can finish it, then that's great."

One of his unfinished projects was a book with the working title *Relative Perspective*. In it, he was exploring how point of view influences perception. "You can have a photograph that has ten people lined up, and one of them is taller than the others. And you'll ask the viewer, 'Is this person tall?' Now, the reality is that you know that person is taller than the other people. But you don't know if they're tall or not. And then you show a photo of that same person with another group of people who are all taller. And you ask the viewer, 'Is that person short?' Well, it's the same person, right?"

The project had tremendous resonance for him as he looked at his own life. "What I'm going through is terrible. I wouldn't wish it on anybody. But there are people who were born without limbs, who were born blind, who were born deaf. And somehow they managed to be successful and lead happy lives, and many have accomplished more than I could ever dream of accomplishing. So from a relative perspective standpoint, I could say, 'Why has God been so good to me? Why am I so lucky?' I met a wonderful girl who's now my wife. I have two great kids. I've had a successful legal career. I have achieved more than I could have been entitled to, based on effort. I've often been lucky and in the right place at the right time."

An intellectual choice to live each day for itself is one thing, and the emotions that color the experiences on any given day are another. At a recent memorial service, he recalled being moved to tears. "It was difficult for me to sit there and realize that, within a year or so, the service is going to be for me, and that casket will have me in it, and it'll be my family and friends here. I looked over at the [deceased's] children and her grandchildren and the grief they were feeling, and I thought, 'What can I possibly do to either spare them that or lessen the pain?' But, then again, I took comfort in that the healing process is part of our DNA, so I'm not as worried as I once was."

Allen also used humor as often as he could to provide levity for his loved ones. On a visit to potential burial plots with Lory and Rabbi Friedman of Temple Israel, he lay down on the candidate plots. "They asked me what I was doing, and I said, 'Well, I'm going to be here for eternity. I want to make sure I have a good view." He crafted an obituary that emphasized his one-night, live music career and recent art pursuits above his thirty-five-year legal career. He contemplated comedic, musical surprises to include in his memorial service.

And then, one day, his life changed again. He and Lory went to the regularly scheduled oncologist appointment. The doctor told them there would be no more treatments. Allen would shift to hospice.

Allen's first impulse was to comfort his doctor. "Dr. Frank would be terrible at poker, I think. His head was down and his shoulders were slumped, and he just had really negative body language. I said, 'Come on, now, doctor. I need you to be strong. I need you at your best.' And he's just looking at me like, 'What's wrong with you? Don't you understand what's happening?' "

But Allen did not, at first. "I had not fully appreciated the demarcation line between going from chemo to hospice," Allen recalled. "I just . . . I didn't view it as a binary moment in my life."

They went to the hospice center they had previously selected, and Allen's confusion persisted. The hospice personnel told him they wanted to keep him overnight for a couple of nights to get his pain medication dosage right. Allen objected, insisting he had been told he didn't have to stay there overnight unless he wanted to. He poured over the admissions forms with all of his legal expertise and raised a series of questions and objections. Finally, he was convinced to sign the forms.

"That's the moment when it hit me that I was crossing a river and this was a real decision, and that, psychologically, there should have been more of a decision process leading up to it. But I was so stupid. I didn't quite get it. So that shook me up."

The disorientation followed him home after the brief stay at the hospice center. "I'm in a totally different place. It's now, 'We know your abdomen is inflated. We know it's hard. Yes, you're losing weight. But we don't care about any of that. We just care if it is causing you pain and what we can do to lessen the pain.' It's a weird sensation. People like to use the term 'the war on cancer.' So we've been fighting the war, and then suddenly I signed a form and the war is over?" In time, he recognized that while the war against cancer would continue, the battle of Allen Wasserman was about to be lost.

"It's the ultimate litmus test because, after I received my diagnosis, I always felt, 'I'm prepared. I fully, mentally understand and have accepted that there's unlikely to be a happy ending here.' Well . . . now I'm going to find out whether I actually had accepted it and whether I do understand. And . . . I think once I got past that moment of being confused about hospice, I shifted. Yeah, I get it. I totally grasp it."

From the start, Allen had decided to be as open as possible with others about his diagnosis so that he didn't have to keep track of who knew what. But now, as word inevitably began to spread about his shift to hospice, he and his family had to reexamine how to manage the rising flood of well-intended attention. "My first response was, 'I don't want a pilgrimage.' But we're still figuring this all out." His sister, Mindy, had arrived to be with him and the family, but he even warned her, " 'I'm not going to spend all my waking hours with you. Sometimes, I'll just sneak away. I don't want to be overwhelmed.' "

In the early days of hospice, Allen was still adjusting to the difference from living with chemotherapy treatments. He could no longer use the same guiding principle of assessing how much energy he had and how best to use it. His condition changed too frequently. It was harder to make decisions.

Lory and Mindy observed that Allen had less energy, and there was increased impairment to his thought processes. They started taking a more overt role in making choices for him, including answering questions directed to him before he could answer. Allen found it frustrating and even demeaning.

"I'm here," he reminded them. "I have most of my faculties. I'm with it. You have to allow me to do the things I can do while I can still do it because otherwise it is very demoralizing."

Allen observed that the entire hospice process is about making decisions related to human dignity. There are constant choices, not just about medical intervention, but about everyday living. "Do you want to live in a care facility or at home? Do you want a nurse to live in your house with you?" The questions keep coming and, with each one, the individual and their family have a chance to define boundaries and try to retain human dignity for as long as possible.

For example, he and Lory recently disagreed over whether to have a hospital bed moved into the house. "I don't want to go upstairs to a hospital bed," Allen said. "At least, I don't want to do it a day before I have to."

While he understood that the instinct of those caring for a loved one in hospice was to make things as easy as possible, Allen believed this could be a mistake. "People should be made aware that you can help with the transition by allowing your loved one to function at . . . the highest level they are capable of functioning at. Don't turn them into the person who needs to have a bib and be fed until they need to be." But he

Allen and wife Lory enjoying some sand and surf together.

acknowledged, "There's no rulebook for this, and inevitably you will get on each other's nerves, despite the best intentions imaginable."

As the conversation wound down, Allen shared that he had recently watched the movie *Awakenings* and become uncomfortable when it came to the scene where the staff is putting a diaper on Robert De Niro's character. "I had to look away. Because that could be me someday."

It was getting harder not to worry about what would happen next. And he might despair at how many days lay ahead or marvel at how many had already passed, depending on the perspective.

Yesterday, Today and Tomorrow [Excerpt]
by Allen C. Wasserman

Rather than dwell on regrets over
the many yesterdays that I cannot have back,
Rather than ponder a future that I
may ultimately lack,

I choose to live for and embrace today . . .
it is the only path over which
I hold any sway.

So each day when I awake,
these simple promises to my family,
my friends and myself I do make.

I promise to accept my yesterdays
without regret or remorse.

I promise not to dwell on the tomorrows
I may never see,

I promise instead to
embrace today, a moment in time
in which I can find peace in
just being me.

Yesterday, today and tomorrow
of all these moments in time
today is eternal
and beautifully sublime . . .

Allen Wasserman passed away on September 1, 2019.

Pamela Parsons Naughton in California (1975).

Weren't We Lucky
• Pamela Parsons Naughton •

by Mary-Lou Weisman

ACTOR, SINGER, DIRECTOR, AND TWO-TIME Tony Award winner James Naughton smiles as he invites me to admire the voluptuous spray of white orchids blooming on the windowsill of his farmhouse in Weston, Connecticut. They were his wife Pamela's passion until she died at home on April 9, 2013 almost seven years ago, after a four-year battle with pancreatic cancer. She was sixty-six years old. While Jim lacks Pam's green thumb, he is proud he has succeeded in keeping those flowers alive.

The life and death of Pamela Parsons Naughton is a remarkable love story. Pam and Jim met at the age of seventeen, dated through college— she at Middlebury in Vermont and he at Brown in Providence. They couldn't get enough of one another.

"She endured nine- and ten-hour bus trips to come down to see me, and I hitchhiked through winter storms to see her."

Pam's curfew required her to be back at Middlebury by Sunday night, but sometimes the lovers couldn't bear to part. That's when Jim would call Pam's housemother, Mrs. Johnston, to explain that Pam wasn't feeling well.

" 'Oh, Jimmy dear, you take good care of Pam. Don't you send her back until she's really feeling better.' " Jim laughs when he remembers. "And I'd say, 'Okay, Mrs. Johnston, thanks a lot.' Pam would stay with me in Providence for a week and then go back to Middlebury and ace all her exams. She was smart. I mean *really* smart."

They married after college and had a son, Greg, while Jim was a graduate student at the Yale School of Drama. Three years later, Keira was born.

Both of their children inherited the drama gene. Keira, an actress and director, is married to Benjamin Forgash, a former film editor who now is a very successful business owner. Their son Greg is an actor, writer, and director, as well as a singer-songwriter with the folk rock band The Sweet Remains. He is married to actress and singer Kelli O'Hara.

Left to right: Jim and Pam Naughton, Kelli O'Hara, and Greg Naughton at the New York Pops concert (2012).

James, Keira, Greg, and I are sitting in the sunroom of their Weston home, talking about Pam—the wife, the mother, the grandmother, and the patient.

"I'm probably going to start crying," Keira says.

Greg beats her to it. "It's been my dumb luck that I was born to this mother and this father. They provided us with an almost sickening amount of love. They were tremendous together, a tremendous team.

"This is rare in any realm—but in the theatrical and artistic world in which they lived, this was particularly rare. Dad's co-stars and colleagues would often take me aside at an opening night party or some other occasion and they'd say, 'Greg, how did your parents do it?' They would lament their many broken marriages and the children who resented them. They wanted insights into the secret of my parents' marriage.

"My mom was a very gentle, shy person, but probably by virtue of the marriage she got herself into, and the lifestyle of being around artists all the time, she became more of an extrovert. Still, I think motherhood was her proudest role. She was the quintessential mother."

Jim recalls that Pam went to college to become a writer. "She was such a private person, the only way she could express herself freely was to write. Then the whole arc of her life began to change; she began to write less and to become more and more of a people person."

"Some years later," Greg says, "when Keira and I were in middle school, she went back to school and got her master's degree in social work, which was certainly the right place for her. At a party or some other event, people would start telling her their life story. They instinctively trusted her. They would confide in her."

Keira laughs. "My mother, the magnet."

"It was unbelievable," Jim adds. "Total strangers would walk up to her. We'd leave a party and she knew about everybody's relationship problems.

"For many decades we lived a charmed life," Jim says, "until an ultrasound confirmed there was a mass in her pancreas." Pam was sixty-two years old. For almost six months, she had been complaining of pressure in her solar plexus.

"She'd take my hand and press it to the spot and ask me if I felt anything. I didn't."

Pam at Weston, CT home (1972).

Several years before, Pam and Jim had both become ill after eating dinner in a favorite theatre district restaurant. Ultimately, Jim's body recovered; Pam's didn't. She wound up with a condition called lymphocytic colitis, an inflammation of the interior lining of the intestine. It was this condition that masked her pancreatic problem. For six months, her doctor mistook the symptoms as being due to the colitis until, finally, he performed an ultrasound.

Pam called Jim from the doctor's office to give him the bad news.

He was in his car, making a turn from his bank onto the Post Road. The moment is seared on his brain.

"I'll never forget that call or the fear that I felt. It was like a stab in the heart.

" 'Come right home, I'll meet you there,' " was all he could say.

Pam, who was strong and tended to underplay her problems, never told Jim that she was going for an ultrasound.

That day, Keira was on her way home from California. "When Dad and Mom and I were together at home, Mom told us that she had been terrified to be alone when the doctor gave her the results of the scan."

The nurse hugged her and asked what she could do to help.

" 'You can write me a prescription for Ativan,' " said Pam, who stopped at the pharmacy before returning home. Because Pam had worked as a social worker at Hall-Brooke Behavioral Health, she knew that Ativan might help to relieve her terror. Later, when Pam tried to wean herself from the drug, Keira tried to talk her out of it.

"Don't feel guilty, Mom. If anybody needs that drug, you do."

In mid-April, the doctor's associate performed an endoscopy, which involved putting a tube down Pam's throat and taking a biopsy specimen from the mass.

The GI doctor assured the Naughtons that the biopsy sample would prove to be benign. He was wrong.

In May, before they received the results of the tests, the family went on a long-planned sailing vacation to Bermuda with friends. That's where Pam received a revised, definitive diagnosis—malignant.

Greg knew right away that her cancer was one of the worst, with one of the lowest survival rates, but he didn't let himself look at the prognosis until after his mother died. "Thinking back," says Greg, "the thing that really surprised me about that vacation is how she seemed carefree and to be having a great time." In fact, had he looked up pancreatic cancer, Greg would have learned that his mother had a fifty percent chance of surviving one year, and a ten percent chance of surviving four years.

"She managed it so well," Keira adds. "She made sure that everybody had a good vacation, that everybody was taken care of."

No one remembers Pam expressing anger when she heard the diagnosis. "I never saw it," Jim says.

Keira remembers that when Pam heard the terrible news, she merely said, "What a crazy turn of events."

"Crazy," indeed, since the substance of the Naughtons' estate plan, drawn up twenty-five years earlier, was predicated on their conviction that Pam would outlive Jim, given the fact that Pam's parents, grandmother, and aunt had all died just a year or two short of one hundred.

Pam got practical. "I want us to go back and talk to our lawyer. We should revisit our whole estate plan."

"Pam soldiered on," said Jim. "Just yesterday, I was thinking about how she dealt with this whole thing for four years. Somehow, she was able never to shed a tear for herself. She never tried to enlist anybody to feel sorry for her. She kept charging on, as if there was nothing wrong."

"There was never a question of whether or not Mom was going to fight it," said Keira. "It was never a debate. Mom was on a mission to buy as much time as possible, and we were going to do whatever we could."

Greg agrees. "She certainly never, ever had a 'woe is me' or a 'why me?' moment—ever."

It seems that Pam skipped the first four of Elizabeth Kübler-Ross' five stages of grief, and instead landed on "acceptance." But she was also going to fight.

"I guess you could say that my mother verged on saintly," Greg adds. "It's a terrible thing to say about somebody who died, because you sound so damn cliché."

Keira chimes in, "One characteristic that kept her from being totally saintly was the fact that she had wicked sense of humor."

Because Pam was deaf in one ear, she often amused the family when she misheard what they'd said. She also had a talent for mixing metaphors. "I'm as deaf as a church mouse," was one of her family's favorites.

"That sent her into fits of giggles," Jim remembers.

Given Pam's nature to turn outward toward others, she focused her attention on the fact that Greg and his wife, Kelli, were about to present her with her first grandchild. For the four years that Pam was to live, Owen would temper her suffering with joy.

Still, like many people who face drastic odds, Pam did try a couple of way-out alternatives. An actor friend advised drinking eight glasses of green tea a day. Greg joined her as an act of solidarity. Another friend from London recommended that she try crystal therapy.

Jim was cautiously un-optimistic. "Yeah, like what have we got to lose?"

"We had long conversations about alternative treatments with the family," Greg said, "and I remember Mom saying, 'Well, the thing is, we've done a lot of thinking about this, we've talked to a lot of people, and the only thing I can tell you is that all the people we know who went the alternative route are not around.' "

A friend advised, "Trust your doctors and stay off the Internet." So now the battle was joined, and it was going to be brutal.

First, Pam endured what might have been a life-saving operation called the Whipple procedure, named after the surgeon who had perfected the technique. The goal was to remove the "head"—about one third of her pancreas—trusting that the cancer was confined to that area. Pam took hope from the fact that a friend who had pancreatic cancer and endured Whipple surgery survived, cancer-free.

Pam at daughter Keira's wedding, with grandson Owen (2011).

The procedure is complicated because the pancreas is located at an intersection of the gallbladder, the duodenum, the stomach, and the bile duct. After the surgery, the doctor sent Pam home, hoping that he had eliminated all the cancer cells—he had not—and that Pam's digestive system would heal and function normally—it did not.

Jim remembers the morning after. "Pam, following directions to get out of bed, walked down the hall while attached to an IV poll rolling along on wheels, somehow smiling at the people we encountered, as if to reassure them that she was just fine. She wasn't."

Pam's body did not recover easily from that operation. Her digestive system rebelled. For almost two months that summer, Jim would hook her up every night through a "port" sewn into her upper chest near her collarbone, attached to a catheter that delivered the nutrients she was not yet able to absorb from ingested food.

"We'd start the twelve-hour drip at around 8 p.m., watch some television, and then I'd move her and the contraption into the bedroom, where she'd sleep with it all hooked up until 8 a.m., until I'd detach her. That's what kept her alive."

Leading the chemo assault was Dr. Richard Frank, head of oncology at Norwalk Hospital's Whittingham Cancer Center. He would come to play an extraordinary role in Pam's care.

Now the ups and downs would begin. One chemo "cocktail" would start to shrink the cancer cells. By way of MRIs or ultrasounds, Dr. Frank would inform them that the cancerous cells were beginning to die.

The Naughtons would ride high on hope for a month or two, until the interior of the cells would stop responding to the medicine and start growing larger again. "And then they'd try her on another one," Jim remembers. "This went on for two and a half years."

"When treatments were working, Rich would be thrilled to deliver the news," Greg recalls.

In addition to the side effects from her treatments, Pam began to suffer from multiple infections from the port, so severe that she was hospitalized three times in the course of several weeks and required a second port to be installed on the other side of her chest.

One night, Jim found her lying on the floor.

" 'Honey, what are you doing?' And I got down on the floor with her and she said, 'What time is it?' and I told her, 'It's 6:30.' And she said, 'What are you doing outside at 6:30 in the morning?' And I put my hand on her forehead, and I was like, oh my God, she has a raging fever, she's hallucinating.

"And we were off to the hospital. Invariably, these infections would happen on a weekend when the hospital labs were closed. They'd give her some kind of blanket antibiotic to get the fever down. Finally, on Monday morning, a lab technician would drop different kinds of antibiotics on cells they'd take from Pam's body, to see which one would work. And then maybe they'd send her home on Tuesday."

On one such weekend, Jim had left the hospital briefly to go home to feed their dogs and find some books to bring to Pam, who was an avid reader. When he returned to Pam's room, he found Dr. Frank sitting next to her bed.

" 'What the heck are you doing here? It's your weekend off. Don't you have to take your kids to soccer games and stuff?' "

To which, Jim reports that Dr. Frank said, " 'When I heard you guys were in here for the third weekend in a row, I had to come by and say hi.' No wonder we all loved him and still do."

Later, as Pam's condition worsened, he would even visit her at home in the mornings on his way to the hospital.

After about two years of treatment, Dr. Frank delivered the bad news that he had tried all the conventional cancer drugs then available. But he also had some qualified good news. He had found a new drug trial in San Antonio, but first she needed to fly there to see if she might qualify. There was only one slot left.

"Pam and I flew down in August. It was one hundred fourteen degrees and blowing. We felt as if we were in a blast furnace. Pam still looked strong and beautiful, so they accepted her. For the next eight months, we went to San Antonio every week. Each Tuesday, we were on the only non-stop flight from JFK to San Antonio. She was treated on Wednesday, and we flew home Thursday morning.

"At first, the new drug's effectiveness looked promising. But then the cancer cells began to rebound and the trial ended for us, and so did our weekly sojourn to San Antonio.

"I don't think we ever really talked much about whether this or that treatment would be effective. My job was to do whatever it took. We had to keep going forward. That's the way she and I were together.

"For three and a half years," Jim added, "you wouldn't have known that she was so sick. She looked wonderful. Even her friends were amazed. She was more fragile and she needed naps, but she looked fine, and her smile made everything worth it."

"Then," Greg adds, "in January of 2013, I think we all noticed a big change, though we were probably loath to voice it."

"January, February, March, and April," Jim confirms, "things really went in the wrong direction. Pam became more fragile. She lost a huge amount of weight and became dependent upon oxygen, morphine pumps, drains, and a phenomenal list of medications that had been keeping her on an even keel. She started to look like somebody who was dying."

By now, Pam was spending more and more time in bed. In response, Jim moved their bedroom into the gym, which was closer to the bathroom and had a big flat screen TV. Jim loaded up three thousand slides of their lives together. Greg, Kelli, Keira, Ben, and Jim would gather around Pam's bed, cocktails in hand, and share a private happy hour of family memories.

Contented moments like these were offset by more suffering. Pam developed a blockage in her bile duct, which required yet another endoscopy and surgical tube to drain the bile. If untreated, the bile would poison and kill her. "That lead to a system of pads and bags," Jim remembers, "so now she's got these things and tape all over the place. Once, in the middle of the night, Pam woke me up and said, 'Jimmy, it's leaking.' So I turned on the lights, and the bag that was supposed to collect the bile had broken open and drained onto the sheets. I changed the bed."

Soon, a social worker, recommended by Dr. Frank, paid the Naughtons a call.

"The three of us sat together in our bedroom, chatting amiably while I wondered what the point of her visit was. Then she explained that her best caregiver had just become available and could move in.

Jim was stunned. "You mean that this woman would come here and live in our house to take care of Pam?"

"Yes," she said. "She's a wonderful woman."

"Well, then," Jim said, "What would *I* do?"

The social worker appeared surprised and looked to Pam, who turned her down gently. "I don't think either of us want someone here in between the two of us."

"I never considered giving over Pam's care to somebody else. I never thought about whether or not I could handle it. It's just one of those things. I didn't know I had it in me. You don't know how you'll be until you get there."

Things went on like this for weeks as Pam continued to lose weight and strength. The family held tight to the hope that things would take a turn for the better again, as they had so many times over the past four years.

"Then Dr. Frank came to the house one day and sat down with Mom alone," Keira remembers. "After he left, Mom told me she had a 'much clearer sense' of where she was and what was happening."

Shortly thereafter, she called a family meeting to deliver what Jim called her "concession speech."

"She called up a local hospice nurse recommended by Dr. Frank, I believe, and had the nurse join, to help her break the news to us and explain how the next stage might go," Greg recalls.

"It was very hard for her to tell us," says Jim, "and it was very hard for me to hear what she had to say: 'Jimmy, we always knew this was a fatal disease.' "

"I really didn't realize how far down the path we were. My role had been to do whatever it took to make it possible to keep going. We had been dealing with extraordinary pressures, but it had become our new normal."

Jim & Pam dancing at a wedding (1999).

There was so much that Pam, the consummate wife, mother, and grandmother, had been looking forward to. Shortly after her diagnosis, her first grandchild had been born. Owen and Pam formed an amazing bond right from the beginning. When he was visiting, Owen preferred the grandmother he called "Baba" over anyone else. Jim called Pam a "baby whisperer."

A couple of years later and deeper into her illness, Charlie was born to Keira and Ben. Pam managed to summon the same amount of devotion and energy for him. One of Pam's great regrets as she drew near the end was that she would not get to welcome her third grandchild, whom Greg and Kelli were expecting a few months later.

The last few weeks, the family stayed very close—Keira, Greg, and their new families traveling back and forth from their New York homes almost daily—and Jim focused exclusively on the elaborate regimen of around-the-clock care that Pam required.

Except once, when the prospect of a tempting movie role required that he leave Pam's side for longer than ever before. The offer came in the form of a phone call from the writer-director David Hare, asking Jim to meet him in New York that week for an interview. Jim had previously read the script of *Worricker* and was enthusiastic about the project. The movie was going to shoot in May or June. The timing seemed right. Jim told Pam about the proposal. "I think this movie might be good for me," he said.

Pam agreed. "When I'm gone, Jim, you have to work."

So with some trepidation, Jim called a registered nurse who lived up the road. For three days, Jim and the nurse rehearsed the intricacies of Pam's care until Jim was confident that she was in good hands.

Nevertheless, he raced to the meeting. "It was down in the damn Village. I parked the car, ran up the stairs, met Hare in the hallway, had a great forty-five minute conversation, got the job, jumped back in the car, and drove home." He'd accomplished the round trip in just under three hours. Pam had slept the entire time.

"Finally, a morning came when Pam woke up, looked at me, and said, 'I don't want to wake up anymore.'

Pam and Jim at the 44th Annual Tony Awards (1990).

"She had fought valiantly for the last four years, but now she was so depleted and totally dependent on all these systems of pain pumps and oxygen tanks and drains.

"I spent the day grappling with what she had said, trying to figure out where I stood, and how I could help her. Later that night, at about eleven o'clock when I got in bed with her, she woke up, looked up at me through her medicated haze, and said, 'Oh, I thought I wasn't going to have to wake up anymore.'

"The realization that she was disappointed to still be alive, that she had gotten there so quickly, was shocking to me. However, given my determination after four years of caring for her to help her in any way I could, I was only too aware that we didn't live in a state where 'dying with dignity'—being able to end your suffering with the help of your physician—was an option. The prospect of Pam suffering in this condition for a long time seemed unbearable to me. Mercifully, her decline was precipitous. She didn't linger."

Two days later, it was clear Pam was near the end. The family, including her three siblings and some close friends, visited her to say their goodbyes.

"A while later, she woke up," says Jim. "She was mostly unconscious at this point. She looked up at me, smiled, and said, 'Weren't we lucky to have found each other when we were just babies?' She gave me that gift, right at the very end."

After that, she receded deeply into unconsciousness. Her family stayed near throughout the day and into the evening, awaiting her last breath. "She had been asleep for hours," Jim says. "I didn't think she was going to come around again. But at 8:30 that night, as all of us were gathered around the bed, she suddenly opened her eyes, sat up briskly, smiled, and looked down at the foot of the bed."

"Kelli and I were standing there, but she wasn't looking at us," says Greg. "She was looking through us."

She started talking with an energy and vivacity that her family hadn't seen for weeks. "Oh, look at you! Aren't you a pretty little girl? You look just like your mommy. What's your name? Is it Charlotte, or am I way off?"

"All of us around the bed had goosebumps," said Greg. "We were like—'What's going on here?' Was she hallucinating? Whatever it was, she was having some kind of experience, and it seemed to be with Kelli's four-month-old fetus. Kelli and I looked at each other."

Kelli said, "Did we ever think of the name Charlotte?"

"No, but I like it," Greg said.

"Me, too," Kelli agreed.

Greg and Kelli had decided not to find out the baby's gender to this point. Instead, they had indulged in considering both girls' and boys' names, constantly changing their minds.

After this event, however, Kelli had a sonogram a day or two later and discovered it was a girl. They named her Charlotte.

"When she finally finished talking to this Charlotte," Jim says about Pam's last conversation, "she lay back down, closed her eyes, and we didn't hear from her again."

Pam passed away shortly before midnight of April 9, 2013. Four years after her diagnosis.

Everyone was exhausted, physically and emotionally. Suddenly, they realized that no one had made any advance plans for what to do with her body. For four long years, no one had wanted to imagine her dying. Now, it was the middle of the night. "Why don't we just go to bed and we'll deal with everything in the morning?" Jim said. But Greg was uncomfortable with the idea.

"Dad had been going and going for such a long time taking care of Mom. He had absolutely nothing left in the tank by the time Mom finally passed away, so I felt a need to help draw things to a conclusion."

Greg called and woke a close friend who had lost his parents recently. He recommended a funeral home in Fairfield, and they managed to get someone on the phone who agreed to come at that hour.

"As we waited for them to arrive, it occurred to me that Mom was still wearing her wedding ring. I removed the ring and handed it to Dad."

Two men arrived sometime after one in the morning to prepare Pam's body. Jim was by her bedside. One of them said to Jim, "Why

167

don't you go into another room so you don't have to watch us take her out?" Jim declined.

"Watching them carry her out of our house was probably the hardest moment of my life, but I thought, 'We've come such a distance together that I have to watch this all the way to the end.'"

It's been six years since Pam died. Charlotte was born September 16 that year—a day after Pam's birthday. When Charlotte turned two, the family found a picture of Pam at the same age and discovered their uncanny resemblance.

Four years after Pam's death, Jim married Sara Sessions, a former dancer with the San Francisco ballet and now a Pilates teacher in Black Rock. Sara Sessions Naughton was heartily welcomed by both families.

"I'm tremendously grateful for that," said Jim. "A friend of mine who loved Pam and has gotten to know Sara, said to me recently, "You know, Jim, you really got lucky twice."

The Naughton family—as close-knit as ever—celebrates Pam's life every year at Christmas in Weston, along with Pam's twin sister and the rest of the Parsons family. In the summers, the Parsons and Naughton families get together at a house on the coast of Maine, a tradition they began over fifty years ago and continue to this day.

Charlie Karp at an album cover shoot at Seagrape in Fairfield, CT (summer 2018).

I Still Love You Anyway
• Charlie Karp •

by Eleanor Duffy

On July 6, 2019, MORE THAN SEVENTY musicians, traveling from as far away as Germany and Nashville, gathered to rock the Levitt Pavilion in Westport, Connecticut in honor of singer, song-writer, and guitarist extraordinaire, Charlie Karp. They played to a sold-out audience of devoted friends and family. And it turned out to be an evening of incredible energy and fun, a joyous send-off for Westport's musical son.

The weather report for July 6 had been ominous; rain and thunderstorms were predicted straight through until 9 p.m. But despite the forecast, around 5:30, the torrential rain that poured all day began to lighten up, and by seven o'clock stopped completely.

This minor miracle must have pleased Brian Keane, Grammy-winning producer and longtime friend of Charlie's. He had recently spent months organizing this tribute concert. In almost biblical fashion, the forecasted thunderstorms ceased, clouds parted, and the show was able to go on. It seemed even the heavens were cooperating that evening, to show their appreciation and love for Charlie Karp.

Five months earlier, on March 10, Charlie passed away. He left this earth peacefully, and I, his humble sister, was blessed and privileged to have been there with him. But when Charlie passed away, his music didn't die. Somehow, it has been reborn to its greater family, the people of Westport who knew and loved him.

I believe the universe conspired to create a musical path for my brother. A combination of genes, luck, and timing swirled together when he was born, and at the young age of sixteen, Charlie found himself with guitar in hand, making albums, appearing in venues across the United States and Europe, and jamming with some of the musical legends he had grown up worshipping. By the time Charlie returned home to Westport at the age of eighteen, he had opened for Jim Morrison and The Doors, was lead guitarist for the Buddy Miles Express, jammed with Ron Wood and Rod Stewart, and played guitar at Jimi Hendrix's funeral, to list just a few of his early accomplishments.

Back on his home turf, Charlie hit the ground running with his own band, White Chocolate, and then The Dirty Angels. There were albums and road trips. But mostly there was incredible, original rock & roll. Charlie's bands played to filled houses throughout the Northeast.

Later, Charlie Karp & The Name Droppers carried the musical banner and Slo Leak was formed with fellow Westporter, Danny Kortchmar. Slo Leak recorded two albums of blues-based rock, which were acclaimed by critics and fans alike, and performed at President Clinton's 1996 Inaugural Ball. They played local gigs, often accompanied by friends Keith Richards and Harvey Brooks. Charlie's musical career turned out to be an amazing study in talent and hope and, also, crushing disappointment. But throughout it all, his love and commitment to Music with a capital "M" never wavered.

When I arrived at Yale New Haven Hospital on March 1, my brother Charlie had been in excruciating pain for two solid weeks. Everything hurt.

I stepped into the east wing elevator and noted how efficiently I seemed to be going about the business of locating Charlie's room, while something sharp up inside my chest was making it hard to breath. I gratefully recognized the first symptoms of "The Zone," where mind and body switch onto automatic pilot, and emotions go AWOL.

I live in Florida. When I got a phone call in early February from our mother, Martha, that Charlie had been admitted to the hospital, I wasn't overly worried. Like the rest of his four siblings, Charlie was in his sixties, at the age when perfect health is no longer taken for granted. Lately, Charlie had been dealing with some cardiac symptoms: arrhythmia and edema, but so far everything was minor and manageable. I assumed/hoped that with a little medication adjustment and diet discipline, he would bounce back like he always did.

But Charlie wasn't bouncing back. The day before I arrived, my mother and sister, Alice, had Charlie transferred to Yale New Haven Hospital. After two weeks of uninformative tests, including an unnecessary colonoscopy, the doctors at the first hospital were still unable to either stabilize Charlie's heart or find any correlation to the severe diarrhea he had been suffering from. When they announced that they were planning to send Charlie home with a bottle of Imodium, my mom and Alice raised hell and moved him to Yale.

The good news was that within twenty-four hours of arriving at Yale New Haven, Charlie finally got a diagnosis. The incredibly bad news: he had cancer. The elevator door opened on the seventh floor, and I felt myself slide further into "The Zone," that surreal state of detachment, of self-protective denial and shock. As I approached Room 708 and opened the door, I thought, *Denial and shock are just what the doctor ordered.*

Because Charlie was in agony. Everything hurt. His cardiac issues, aggravated by the cancer, made it impossible for him to be properly treated for pain. Serious pain meds interfered with efforts to stabilize his heart: his blood pressure plummeted scarily while his heartrate simultaneously shot through the roof. So, for the past two weeks, because of this medical complication and the first hospital's inability to diagnose what was wrong with him, Charlie had been treated for stage 4 liver cancer with Tylenol.

One-year-old Charlie with mother, Martha, in Mount Vernon,
NY (fall 1953).

When I entered his room, I immediately understood why he hadn't been able to speak with me when I had called. Why my sister had broken down on the phone and sobbed desperately to my father. Why my mother had become shut down. Everything was hurting Charlie. He didn't even smile when he saw me standing there in his doorway. I navigated around the medical paraphernalia crammed in the crowded hospital room, sat down in a chair next to his bed, and carefully held onto one of his hands.

Charlie's hands were a thing of wonder, the connection to his guitar, which anyone who ever met him knew was his raison d'être. Charlie never simply held a guitar, he melded with it. The body of the guitar fit with his own, and his hands supported the neck. Then his long, slim fingers, trained by a lifetime of fingering, strumming, dreaming and escaping, became the hammers and keys that made the notes.

When we were very young, Charlie would practice his guitar so hard and so constantly that his fingers would actually bleed. And then he would continue playing on anyway. Ours was not a happy home, and it was as though Charlie tuned out all the discord and dysfunction with his music. He was always playing. If you wanted to talk to him, you had to interrupt some riff, and then even as he conversed, he'd keep on doodling on his guitar. He played every day until he got ordered to put his instrument down and eat dinner, played when he was supposed to be doing his homework, even played while he was watching TV. He spent endless hours figuring out fingering, teaching his fingers to fly and dance along the neck of his guitar.

Charlie's affinity for music did not come out of the blue. There was musical DNA on our mother's side: Walter Damrosch, the conductor of the New York Philharmonic, was a great-cousin, who debuted George Gershwin's "American in Paris." Our mom played acoustic guitar and had a beautiful singing voice. Our dad, Marshall, was an avid fan of

Dixieland, ragtime, jazz, and European musicians Django Reinhardt, Edith Piaf, and Lotte Lenya. Marshall played his great record collection on a special Hi-Fi system that no one, including my mother, was allowed to touch. Growing up, there was always music in our house.

Charlie at eight years old on a family vacation (1961).

When Charlie was ten, our mom signed him up for guitar lessons at the YMCA with another schoolmate. The two boys had a friendly competition, and I remember how crushed Charlie was when his friend got an electric guitar first, for Hanukkah, and Charlie had to wait an extra week until Christmas.

But he did get it. The red Hagstrom with three pick-ups that had been in the window of The Melody House shop on Main Street. At the time, even I knew it was a good thing Charlie got that guitar, because he more than just wanted it. He needed it. He plugged it into the amp on Christmas morning, and it's not much of an exaggeration to say that he was never without a guitar in his hands again.

On that Hagstrom, Charlie taught himself the chords to "Wipeout," "Walk, Don't Run," "Pipeline," and all the Ventures' records, which he played on our dad's forbidden stereo while he was at work. Later, when Charlie was fourteen, he also "borrowed" our father's forbidden Daimler sports car to drive across town and pick up another friend. Somehow, Charlie knew he was not bound by rules the rest of us had to obey. At that young age, Charlie was out of the house most of the time, practicing and playing real gigs for money, and already knew without a doubt what he wanted to do for the rest of his life.

Charlie's musical journey was shared by many people. But growing up with Charlie gave me a different perspective on some well-known events. For example, the story behind his song, "I Still Love You Anyway." Charlie wrote it for his first girlfriend, Debbie Sims. Many people know this. But I was there eavesdropping the Saturday night in 1969, when sixteen-year-old Charlie was on the phone being told by a friend that Debbie had seen him play at the Staples High School dance and thought he was cool. Our dad had given Charlie a pair of white Gucci loafers, which Charlie wore to the gig. Finding out that Debbie liked him, Charlie was so happy he gushed to his friend, "It was the shoes, man! Fashion talks! Fashion talks!"

Charlie might be a little embarrassed now to have this teenage story told. But it was so quintessentially Charlie, sweet and cool at the same time. He'd forgive me for sharing it.

Later, after Charlie left high school to go on tour, Buddy Miles recorded "I Still Love You Anyway" for the *Them Changes* album. Coming from R&B singer Buddy, the lyrics "I could be sad and crying and my brother would wonder why" had a certain meaning. But I know these words were literally about our brother Tommy, who was thirteen at the time and shared a bedroom with Charlie in our house on Green Brier Road. Tommy *had* wondered why Charlie was crying when his heart got broken.

In July 1970, our dad called to let us know Charlie was going to be on TV. The Buddy Miles Express was performing on an American

Charlie at seventeen years old (1970).

Bandstand spin-off. First, the whole twelve-piece band played the tune "Them Changes," which was on the charts. And then it was just Charlie alone, sitting on a stool by himself with his acoustic guitar, and Buddy, singing Charlie's song. By this time, Charlie was all of seventeen years old. Watching him capably doing his job, playing his own sincere, sweet love song on national television, I was incredibly proud of him. But I also realized this: Charlie belonged there more than he had ever belonged at home with us.

There was something about Charlie, something more than his talent, setting him apart. He had an inner confidence that, at its core, had nothing to do with his ego. Charlie was born with a gift, and he simply unwrapped and claimed it.

After such a propitious beginning, maybe there was no place Charlie could have gone but down. For many reasons, some obvious in hindsight, others still heart-wrenchingly arbitrary, the trajectory of Charlie's musical career took a turn.

The biggest problem was Charlie's drinking. It was the 1970s, and many of us were fully immersed in the "sex, drugs, and rock 'n' roll" culture of the time. I, myself, had become one of Charlie's most constant drinking partners. For two years, when Charlie let our sister Alice and me sing with his band, we spent a lot of time together, making demos, playing gigs, and partying.

By the early 1980s, our partying had become a problem. Along with musical DNA, we also inherited the alcoholic gene. In 1982, by the grace of God, I wandered into AA and got sober. And then, with misguided good intentions, showed up at Charlie's house like Church Lady, carrying pamphlets and giving sermons about how he was sabotaging himself with booze. It didn't go over well. By 1985, Charlie and I had a major falling out, and did not see each other often for many years.

Charlie opening for Aerosmith at Boston Gardens.

179

Leading up to his problems with alcohol, Charlie had some impressive accomplishments coupled with sickening setbacks. One of the most dramatic was in 1978, when Charlie was twenty-five years old: The Dirty Angels recorded their second album on A&M Records. There was huge excitement and support from the record company. PR was in full swing, and a summer tour had been booked for the band to open for Aerosmith. It seemed that everything was on track for The Dirty Angels' success. But a week before the album was due to be released, Charlie's appendix burst. He spent two painful weeks in the hospital, and then two more at home continuing to recover. Everything had to be cancelled. The record came out with no promotion, and bombed. The blow to Charlie's career and to his morale was devastating.

In the face of this disaster, Charlie's already overly-friendly relationship with alcohol became an unhealthy dependency, and eventually turned into a classic conundrum: were the setbacks causing Charlie to drink, or was his drinking causing the setbacks? After a while, there was no clear answer. Charlie was caught in a vicious cycle that he never fully escaped.

In the years that followed, Charlie went through hard times, financially and emotionally. But no matter how bleak things got, he never considered giving up on music. To make a living he recorded national TV ads and sang vocals for commercials like, "I like eggs, from my head down to my legs" (one of my favorites). And he began to give guitar lessons to lucky Westporters.

It was during this period that he also recorded the Slo Leak albums with Danny Kortchmar. And he worked on projects with longtime friend, Coleytown Junior High classmate Brian Keane, winning an Emmy for their soundtrack on an ESPN Basketball Special. These odd jobs buoyed him through the tough times and led him in a new direction.

With a financial investment from one of his weekend-warrior students, a hedge fund executive, Charlie was able to build a recording studio in his house. There, he began to work with his students and other musicians recording their original songs as well as his own.

From then on, Charlie's home became a hotbed of creativity. His driveway was filled with cars, his studio occupied with students, engineers, percussionists, and vocalists. The music was constant, from beginners' lessons, to songwriters' demos, to local legends jamming.

And Charlie continued doing what he loved most, playing his guitar. He played charity events, reunions, and always had a regular gig at some local club, where he would perform original material, classics, and especially the blues, with the current version of his latest band. No matter the event, when he was on stage playing, it was always clear by Charlie's smile that he was doing what he was put here to do.

Like all of us, Charlie got older and had to make peace with the fact that his big chance at fame and fortune had passed. There seemed to be something extra hard, though, for Charlie, having had such potential and coming so close to fulfilling it. Life became real for Charlie in a way that he wasn't prepared for. And that none of us, at the time, understood.

Charlie with Herb Worthington (1978).

I, for one, thought I knew for sure Charlie needed to quit drinking. I've since come to see that sometimes when life appears to be going horribly wrong, it is actually going exactly right. For example: his burst appendix may have saved Charlie from the fate of some of his more famous associates. At the time, he was messing around with bad drugs, and on New Year's Eve 1975 overdosed on heroin. He was saved by his friends' CPR and call for an ambulance. I wonder now if Charlie's career hadn't been derailed then, if he had achieved the success he seemed destined for, whether he might have died at a much younger age like his idol Jimmy Hendrix. In this way and others, Charlie's path was wrought with apparent missteps that may have actually been saving graces. His overdose itself might have been one of these weird blessings, scaring Charlie into sticking with less lethal anesthesia.

And that's what, I now understand, Charlie's drinking was about. Anesthesia. It allowed him to weave all his heartbreak and disappointment into what had become the tapestry of his life, in order to carry on. I had caused Charlie a lot of pain by nagging and judging him about his drinking when we were younger. Luckily, a number of years ago, I figured this out enough to apologize for hurting him. And Charlie, being Charlie, had already forgiven me.

By the time I arrived at Yale New Haven Hospital on March 1 and took hold of Charlie's hand, my mom and sister Alice had been there for more than two weeks. After the initial diagnosis of cancer, it took the cardiac and oncology teams at Yale a week to determine Charlie's overall condition and medical options. Charlie had been told of his diagnosis and, even though he was in horrible pain, was stoically waiting to begin treatment. He wanted to get better. But two days didn't pass in a row when Charlie rallied or even stayed the same. Without the experts telling us, we began to understand that what we feared most was unfolding.

At the same time, something else was beginning to reveal itself. Another one of life's mysterious twists: Charlie being suspended in this terrible limbo gave rise to a tremendous outpouring of love, prayers, and good wishes. He was well-liked, and many people wanted to reach out and support him. It started with visits and calls from his friends, but quickly turned frenetic.

A steady stream of people began getting off the elevator, inundating the nurses' station with requests for directions to his room. The phone by Charlie's bed rang off the hook. One of the nurses, exasperated and awestruck after a scuffle with one of Charlie's friends, came rushing down the hall and asked me, "Charlie Karp, who is he? Is he famous?"

There was something amusing about this "rockstar" treatment. But intrusive and hard, too. Charlie was barely strong enough to hold the receiver to his ear, never mind hold court with throngs of people. We made a point to let him know about everyone who showed up or reached out, and tried to let him make the decision himself whether he was up to talking with them. At the beginning, Charlie believed he was going to get better and thought he would have time, later on, to catch up with his friends. Once we began to realize that there would be no "later on," Charlie was simply too sick to see anyone. But the wave of appreciation and love kept coming. It was unstoppable.

As stressed out as we were, my mom, Alice, and I began to see that this groundswell for Charlie was some kind of phenomenon. Charlie, preparing to leave us, had set something in motion. We felt protective of him, but did our best to let in the power of this positive wave coming towards him. After one to-do in the hall with someone disappointed at not being able to see him, Charlie said to me, "It does make me feel good that people love me." He was aware of it all and it raised his spirits.

On Thursday, March 7, my mom, Alice, and I were summoned to the family meeting with Charlie's doctors. We were told that Charlie was too sick to withstand any treatment for his cancer. Barring a miracle, there would be no meaningful recovery for him.

Ironically, the hopelessness of Charlie's situation might have given us some strange relief. Since there were no other options, the excruciating decision to let nature take its course had been made for us. And, finally, Charlie's pain could be treated.

But we still had to tell him. We had to tell our cool, sweet, amazing Charlie that he was dying.

Dr. Nancy Kim, Charlie's attending physician, offered to help us. On Friday morning, we gathered at Charlie's bedside. I can't remember many details, being by this time fully launched into "The Zone." Just that Dr. Kim was kind, and at the same time completely honest. She explained the situation to him, and when Charlie asked her, point-blank, "Am I dying?" she answered, "Yes, you are. I'm so sorry." Not surprisingly, upon hearing this, the first words out of Charlie's mouth were: "What about my music?"

While the rest of us were sobbing, Charlie told the doctor about his studio, about his "joy" creating music there. His greatest concerns were the unfinished recording projects of his students and band-mates.

Mom was sitting closest to him, and Charlie turned to her and asked, "What do you think, Mumsy?" And she could only answer: "I think you are going to be loved."

But Charlie was already loving us right back with his humor and courage. Immediately following this meeting, my mother and I made an excuse to leave the room, saying we were going for coffee. As we left, Charlie with his typical wit, said, "Coffee? Well, guzzle up." His care had been changed from medical to palliative, and Alice was there when the nurse came in to finally administer a gigantic dose of morphine. Alice said she could actually see Charlie's pain lessen as his face and body relaxed. Grateful to observe his moment of peace, Alice said, "Charlie, you look toasted." And Charlie responded, "With butter."

Later that day, one of Charlie's friends evaded the hospital security we had requested and was suddenly outside his door. Like always when anyone showed up, we asked Charlie if he wanted to see this person, and Charlie answered matter-of-factly, "I'm dying here. I can't see him." His tone wasn't one of self-pity or anger. He was just busy with something important, preparing to leave this earth, and wasn't available for small talk. Maybe it was because he was so worn out and sick; Charlie didn't seem to spend any time at all resisting his verdict. He started, right away, to let go.

That day, after Dr Kim's visit, our brother Tommy came to the hospital and sang to Charlie The Righteous Brothers' "Rock and Roll Heaven." Charlie and Tommy had a complicated relationship and didn't see each other often. But one of the good things our family was always able to do, when we did get together, was make music. Throughout the years, we would sit around the kitchen table, Charlie would play guitar, figure out the background vocals, and make us all sound fabulous. Those sessions were heaven. Tom, in particular, has a terrific voice and I think by singing, he was telling Charlie that nothing else mattered now.

And Charlie agreed. He kissed Tom and told him he loved him. Our father Marshall, who lives in Florida, called and spoke to Charlie. We could only hear Charlie's side of the conversation as he said over and over, "I love you too, man." And finally, "Who knows? Maybe something will happen, maybe there will be something we can do." When Charlie handed me back the phone, he said, "Marshall is really unhappy." It was just like Charlie to be sorry he was hurting Marshall, and even to fib a little about the possibility of him getting better, in order to ease his father's pain.

Our mom is in fragile health and my sister had heroically been holding down the fort since Charlie first entered the hospital. Once I arrived, Alice and I formed a relay, taking turns to make sure someone was always with him.

That Friday night, Alice stayed with Charlie. I arrived early Saturday morning to relieve Alice, and found that they both had a rough night. There was loud disturbance from another patient down the hall. Charlie was given a sedative, along with his pain medication. I settled in the chair next to his bed.

Charlie with brother Tommy in Wilton, CT (1976).

Later that day, Charlie needed to be put on a morphine drip, and from then on he appeared to be sleeping soundly. The hospice nurse instructed me he could still hear everything; he was aware on some level. She also let me know that Charlie's moment of departure was coming soon. I felt very alone and scared.

I'm not religious, but I reached out for the hospital chaplain. She came to Charlie's room, and I told her how I was feeling. She asked me what I was afraid of, and I said, out loud in Charlie's presence, "I'm afraid of how much it's going to hurt when he leaves."

The chaplain pointed out that even though I was afraid, I was still there. And by being there, I was letting Charlie know how much I loved him. That made me grateful for the fluke in timing that allowed me to be the one to be with him. I reached out and took Charlie's hand again.

Since I knew he could hear, I tried to sing to him "Danny Boy," and one of our favorite songs from when we were little, "My Little Lady," a Jimmie Rodgers tune from our dad's record collection. When the hospice nurse came in, I let go of Charlie's hand so she could take his pulse. She said, "His hands are so warm." When I asked what the significance of that was, she said it meant he probably wasn't quite ready to go. As soon as she left the room, I grabbed hold of his hand again. Then I heard my cell phone beep and this text from Brian Keane was posted to me and Alice:

"After the Reunion Band fundraiser last night, that Charlie was supposed to play with us on, I posted a heartfelt, loving tribute to Charlie on my Facebook page. I focused my tribute on Charlie's great musical legacy, and invited people to share their thoughts and memories about Charlie, and how much he has meant to them.

"The response has been truly overwhelming. Charlie has so many fans, musical collaborators, friends, and people who love him, it is really inspiring.

"In less than 24 hours, there has been an outpouring of literally hundreds of loving responses, and over 70 shares. This has spurred all kinds of postings of Charlie's various other musical accomplishments elsewhere as well, and powerful testimonials to Charlie, his music, and how important he has been in people's lives.

"I hope Charlie has some sense of how widely he and his music are loved. If he got better by some miracle, he could probably sell out any place he played. I love the guy too, but he knows that. Sending my love (can't say "thoughts and prayers" any more). Hope at the very least, that you can find some comfort in the outpouring of love for Charlie and his musical legacy."

I was so happy to be able to read this message to Charlie. I sat and "discussed" it with him.

It was almost midnight, and I told Charlie that I would stay right there and was going to close my eyes. I leaned back in the reclining chair next to his bed. But before I settled in, I decided to sit back up and read Brian's text to Charlie again. As I read, I was sharply aware of the labored way Charlie was breathing now, and of the fine, smooth skin on his wonderful, still warm hand.

I must have dozed off. When I woke, the room was dark and quiet and Charlie was gone. It wasn't quite 1 a.m. I realized later that I had only been asleep for a brief time. And even though he might have stayed longer, Charlie slipped away during that short interval. Knowing I was scared, maybe he decided to leave then because he wanted to spare me. It was just the kind of thing he would do. Charlie died like the prince that he was.

⚜

Charlie's memorial service, held on March 30, was an invitation only affair, organized by friends Mark Soboslai, Brian Keane, and Bonnie Erickson. Mark reserved the funeral home. Brian arranged the music: a live acoustic set of three guitarists, and a "soundtrack" of Charlie's songs. Bonnie collected and mounted a fantastic array of photos, chronicling Charlie's fifty-year musical career.

There needed to be a guest list because it had become clear from the flood of memories, videos, and Charlie stories on social media that an open forum might turn into a mob scene. Bonnie took charge and made sure that everyone who was important to Charlie was invited. And everyone came.

Charlie would have loved it. Filled to capacity with people from every era of his life, it was like taking a trip in a time machine. Charlie remained in Westport, and it says something about a person to have so many people who knew him "when" consider him to be one of their best friends. Some of these old friends traveled far and wide to be there. Charlie's boyhood cohort, Charles Parriot, flew from the Czech Republic. And Charlie's own best friend, David Hull, came from Boston to give part of the eulogy. David, now a member of Aerosmith, was Charlie's bass player and musical partner throughout much of his life. When they were both teenagers, they went on the road together with Buddy Miles, and then formed White Chocolate and The Dirty Angels. David, who has since had an illustrious career of his own, said, "I doubt I will ever play with a greater guitar player than Charlie." And, "Here's to the best musician I ever knew, and the best friend I ever had."

And Charlie's "newer" friends, the ones he had been teaching, recording, and playing with for the past twenty years, were there in force as well. When it was my turn to speak, I was able to tell these great friends of Charlie that, although I had only met some of them in passing, I felt like I knew them. Whenever I visited, Charlie would drag me down to his studio and play me the pieces he was working on. It truly was his joy. He loved his friends and their songs. They made him very happy.

Because of the wonderful music that was played, the reunion with old friends and new, and the love and sharing that went on, Charlie's funeral unfolded to be an exuberant celebration. At the end, as per Brian's arrangement, Charlie's song "Giving It All I Got" started to play, and in keeping with the spirit of the service, I jumped out of my seat and began to dance. To my delight, a whole bunch of the congregation joined me, and we all rocked out to Charlie's upbeat, awesome tune. It was so great. Charlie would have loved it!

The outpouring of love and appreciation for Charlie from the people of Westport continues. The Levitt Pavilion has hosted many famous, accomplished performers over the years. But the number of people who bought tickets for the Charlie Karp Tribute Concert broke all attendance records. (The previous record was held by Charlie's Reunion Band show two years earlier).

Clearly, Charlie is still Westport's favorite. A dressing room there has been named for him, and the stage at The Seagrape Cafe in Fairfield, where Charlie played a weekly gig for the past five years, has also been dedicated to him. Discussions are ongoing about whether to place a Charlie Karp Memorial Bench somewhere in downtown Westport or at Compo Beach. And there are two documentaries in the works, one about Charlie's life and career, and one about the amazing Tribute Concert this past July.

Most wonderful of all, the Charlie Karp Memorial Fund was founded by Charlie's friends, Rafe Klein and Bruce Carter. It is a scholarship to benefit a promising young Fairfield County musician every year. Individual contributions, plus the proceeds from the Tribute Concert, have already exceeded expectations. And generous donations of studio time from Carriage House Recording Studios of Stamford and Horizon Recording Studio of West Haven have been added to the fund.

Finally, Charlie's last album *Back To You* was released on June 7 by Red Parlor Records.

The universe conspired to create a musical path for my brother Charlie. And his death is turning out to be just one step along that road. Instead of an ending, it seems to be the start of a larger context from which Charlie's life and legacy are being launched anew. Fresh recognition of his great talent and the generous way he shared himself and his music have become clear now in a way that was not possible while his legacy was still forming.

"Charlie Karp" could have been a household name all over the world, not just in Westport. He really was that good. But despite, or maybe because of, the genes, luck, and timing that set him on the path to fame and fortune, he ended up needing to figure out a different way to keep playing his guitar.

And he did. And he made many of his fellow Westporters very happy in the process. Charlie lived to be sixty-five years old, doing what he was born to do, with the people who really knew and loved him. The ones who came to his memorial service and the 1,800 others honoring him at the Levitt Pavilion weren't just fans, they were his friends. Many knew him his whole life.

In the big scheme of things, that makes him the greatest success in the world. Like Harry Bailey at the end of "It's A Wonderful Life," I lift my glass and say:

To my brother, Charlie Karp, the richest man in town.

In Memoriam

by Marsha Temlock
(7/13/2019)

At the dock you furled the jib
Secured the main
Ship-shaped the deck
Before heading home.

Three years gone.
Three years lost,
Your ashes flotsam
Silt on memory's waves

The wind has died
The sails have luffed
I scatter petals in your wake
The anchor buried in my heart
The stays still chime your name.

Cover Artist

REGARDLESS OF HOW SOBERING AND serious the subject matter might be, for me the cover of any book still has to have strong visual appeal. How to achieve that with a book on death and dying?

I started with a neutral black background because fifty-four square inches (6x9) of any other color might prompt a reflexive emotional response, like joy or even sadness. Instead, I wanted to guide the viewer to a more thoughtful place. Using a formal but colorful font against the black background gave the cover some of the sophistication and visual appeal I was looking for, but little else.

Staring at it over a period of days, the blackness behind the lettering began to suggest a great void, yearning to be filled, but with what? Perhaps a faded family photo or a page from a diary. *Too flat and specific,* I thought. What if it was something more universal and compelling, like the night sky?

I recalled hearing a song with "shooting star" in the lyrics and thought it might give me some guidance. Instead, I came across this quote attributed to a little-known writer named Nahiar Ozar that said it all, and made a shooting star virtually impossible to avoid as the "star" of the cover.

"In your life you will meet shooting stars. You will see them, make your wish and see them disappear."

—Miggs Burroughs

Miggs Burroughs

A lifelong resident of Westport, Miggs Burroughs has created award-winning graphics for commercial and nonprofit clients throughout Fairfield County and beyond, including the Westport Town Flag, four covers for *TIME Magazine* and a U.S. postage stamp. Miggs is co-founder of Artists Collective of Westport and was the Westport Library's first artist-in-residence.

Authors

Eleanor Duffy

Eleanor was in second grade when the Karp family moved to Westport, CT in 1961. She attended Coleytown Elementary and Junior High Schools, and graduated from Staples in 1972. Eleanor went to college in New York City and eventually met her love, Peter Duffy. In 1985, she and Peter married in Shanghai, China. They traveled the world, had many great adventures, the best being the birth of their wonderful son Peter Joseph Duffy in 1993. Presently, Eleanor lives in Florida and, at the age of sixty-five, is finally becoming what she always wanted to be: a writer.

Sarah Gross

Sarah Gross is a Westport, Connecticut powerhouse who emerged at the forefront of the organic food movement over thirty years ago. She founded Cabbages & Kings, a highly successful catering company, and has worked for high-profile clients including Martha Stewart, President Bill Clinton, and President Barack Obama. In 2015, she opened C&K Community Kitchen, a certified commercial incubator kitchen, which hosts local start-ups creating organic, non-GMO products. An advocate for locally sourced organic ingredients, she strongly supports Bionutrient, regenerative farming.

Her creativity extends beyond the kitchen, and she's had paintings featured in galleries such as the Silvermine Arts and Kripalu Centers. In addition, she is a somatic-oriented trauma healer trained in pre- and peri-natal birth education, Somatic Experiencing® and various other modalities, working primarily with tuning forks as a form of energetic processing.

Frank Hall

Frank Hall is Minister Emeritus of The Unitarian Church in Westport, where he served as Senior Minister from 1984 until 2013. He started his professional life as a teacher before beginning his ministerial career in 1970 in Lexington, Massachusetts while in seminary. Ordained in 1972, he then served the Murray Unitarian Universalist Church in Attleboro, Massachusetts for twelve years. A published poet himself, Frank created a poetry anthology with audio accompaniment, *Natural Selections: Sacred Poems Chosen and Read* by Frank Hall. A proud great-grandfather, Frank resides in Westport, Connecticut with his wife Lory Nurenberg and their mini-labradoodle Parker.

Sheryl Kayne

Sheryl Kayne is the author of five books in Westport Library's collection: *Immersion Travel USA: The Best & Most Meaningful Volunteering, Living & Learning Excursions,* recipient of the Society of American Travel Writers Foundation's Lowell Thomas Travel Journalism Award in Best Travel Guidebook category; and *Volunteer Vacations Across America,* named on Amazon's List of Best New Travel Books. Her children's books include *Queen of the Kisses, Queen of the Kisses Meets Sam Under a Soup Pot*, and *Scary States of Mind: Terror in Texas.* She's currently at work on a series of domestic thrillers, cozy mysteries, and non-fiction on How to Raise Confident Writers. You can find more information at www.sherylkayne.com and SherylKayne@gmail.com.

Jarret Liotta

A native of Westport, Jarret gratefully enjoys his career as a freelance writer, photographer and filmmaker. His essays and articles have appeared in over 100 publications, his fiction has received awards, and he's written content for many businesses and nonprofits. He's also a busy photojournalist, publishing dozens of pictures each week, and an accomplished video producer. Jarret was thrilled to be part of *In Death, the Gift of Life* and hopes readers are inspired to delve a little deeper into their preconceptions about death and dying . . . Let's strive to have no fear!

Diane Meyer Lowman

Diane's essays have appeared in many publications, including *O, The Oprah Magazine, Brain, Child, Brevity Blog*, and *When Women Waken*. She writes a weekly column called "My Life on the Post Road" for *Books, Ink* (books.hamlethub.com/booksink/local-writers/). In addition to essays, she has written a memoir called *Nothing But Blue*, which was published in November 2018 by She Writes Press. Shortly thereafter, she received her M.A. in Shakespeare Studies from the University of Birmingham's Shakespeare Institute. She has explored other forms of literary expression in more than 1,500 haiku (Lotus922.wordpress.com) and essays analyzing each of Shakespeare's thirty-seven plays (DiLo922.wordpress.com). In July 2019, she was named Westport, CT's first Poet Laureate.

Diane also teaches yoga, provides nutritional counseling, and tutors Spanish. She holds a PhD in Wholistic Nutrition and a black belt in Tae Kwon Do.

Jonah Newman

Jonah Newman is a Brooklyn-based writer, artist, and editor. He has written, illustrated, and self-published a graphic novel and many short comics, and is currently working on a graphic memoir. Professionally, he is an assistant editor at Scholastic, where he works on picture books and graphic novels, including Dav Pilkey's Captain Underpants and Dog Man series. When he's not drawing, reading, or editing graphic novels, he binges history podcasts and gets way too invested in his fantasy baseball team. His grandmother, Estelle Margolis, taught him that love is all that matters.

Lory Nurenberg

Lory Nurenberg serves on the faculty at Sacred Heart University School of Social Work. Prior to her current position, Lory worked in hospice care for ten years at Vitas Healthcare. Her social work career has ranged from psychotherapist in private practice to Executive Director of a family service agency. She has developed and led countless presentations and workshops and is a state-certified Divorce Mediator. Lory also has a background in the arts, starting her professional career as an actress and voiceover performer. She resides in Westport, Connecticut with her husband Frank Hall and their mini-labradoodle Parker.

Craig D.B. Patton

Craig D. B. Patton lives in a 200-year-old house in Westport, CT and writes in what used to be the toll taker's office. His published works include short stories, poems, scripts, flash, micro fiction, drabbles, tweets, and other things made out of words. He is a social media consultant specializing in LinkedIn and helps professionals, companies, and organizations tell their story. His volunteer work includes serving

5+ years as the Scoutmaster of Scouts BSA Troop 36, where he received the Unit Leader Award of Merit. He is also on the board of Friends of Sherwood Island State Park and contributes to the marketing and programming of Saugatuck Congregational Church, UCC where his wife is the pastor.

Marsha Temlock

Marsha Temlock is the author of *The Exile* and *Your Child's Divorce: What to Expect, What You Can Do*. She is a retired English teacher at NCC. Proud resident of Westport, she is delighted to be represented in the Westport Library book and to celebrate her husband Stephen Temlock who volunteered as a job coach for many years, helping executives in their career search.

Robin Weinberg

Robin Weinberg produces participatory multimedia oral history projects for communities and nonprofits that harness the power of people's stories and experiences to build understanding, especially across difference.

With an MA in Oral History, she founded an organization that helps cancer patients record their life stories, works with nonprofits on using oral history for marketing and fundraising, conducts interviews, designs project websites, and teaches oral history to students of all ages.

Most recently, she launched WestportVoices (www.westportvoices.com), a local multimedia conversation and storytelling project designed to record interviews and illuminate voices from across Westport's diverse population.

In her free time, she plays racquet sports, bakes and decorates elaborate cakes for family and friends, and is learning, quite horribly, to play the harp, while her husband and three daughters unconvincingly tell her how great it's going.

Mary-Lou Weisman

Mary-Lou Weisman is an award winning journalist (*The Atlantic Monthly*) and bestselling author, *My Middle-Aged Baby Book*. Her other published works include *Playing House in Provence: How Two Americans Became a Little Bit French* (iUniverse); *Al Jaffee's Mad Life* (Harper Collins), *Traveling While Married* (Algonquin Books) and *Intensive Care: A Family Love Story* (Random House). Her essays, feature articles, interviews, and film and book reviews have appeared in many magazines, among them *The New Republic, Newsweek,* and *Vogue.* For several years, she wrote personal essays, articles and travel essays for the *New York Times.* She has also served as a commentator on Public Radio International. She is a member of Phi Beta Kappa, PEN, and the Authors Guild. She had taught memoir and personal essay writing at the Tisch School at NYU and The New School University. She currently teaches both disciplines at the Westport Library. She is married to Larry Weisman.

Dan Woog

Native Westporter Dan Woog is a writer, blogger—and the Staples High School boys soccer head coach. He has written 17 books, and been published in the *New York Times, Sports Illustrated,* and *USA Today.* His hyperlocal blog, "06880" (tagline: "Where Westport meets the world") draws more than 10,000 unique visitors a day. His "Woog's World" column has run in the *Westport News* since 1986. Dan has won national writing awards for his coverage of soccer, and LGBT issues. His business clients have included IBM, Monster.com and Tauck World Discovery.

For more information about the authors,
please visit the Fairfield Scribes' website at
www.fairfieldscribes.com.